SCHOLASTIC News Leveled Informational Texts

GRADE 4

New York • Toronto • London • Auckland • Sydney
Mexico City • New Delhi • Hong Kong • Buenos Aires

Photos ©: cover left: David Jon/NordicPhotos/Getty Images; cover top center: Stepan Kapl/Shutterstock; cover right: Tim Graham/Getty Images; cover bottom center: Michael Krinke/iStockphoto; cover bottom right: Andrew Aitchison/Corbis/Getty Images; back cover bottom left: Stepan Kapl/ Shutterstock; back cover bottom right: Michael Krinke/iStockphoto; 3 left: Business Wire/Getty Images; 3 right: Library of Congress; 6 and throughout: Andrew Aitchison/Corbis/Getty Images; 12 and throughout: Jennifer Pottheiser; 13 and throughout: Richard Theis/EyeEm/Getty Images; 14 and throughout: Jennifer Pottheiser; 21 and throughout: Rawpixel.com/Shutterstock; 27 and throughout: Javier Larrea/Getty Images; 33 and throughout: Mark Edward Harris/Getty Images; 45 and throughout: Library of Congress/Getty Images; 46 and throughout: Library of Congress; 51 and throughout: Keystone-France/Getty Images; 57 and throughout: Ethan Miller/Getty Images; 69 top right and throughout: Ralph White/Getty Images; 69 bottom left and throughout: Dorling Kindersley/Getty Images. Maps by Jim McMahon, Scholastic Inc.

Editor: Maria L. Chang
Cover design by Michelle H. Kim
Interior design by Kay Petronio

Scholastic Inc., 557 Broadway, New York, NY 10012
ISBN: 978-1-338-28474-4
Copyright © 2019 by Scholastic Inc.
All rights reserved.
Printed in the U.S.A.
First printing, January 2019.

2 3 4 5 6 7 8 9 10 40 25 24 23 22 21 20

Table of Contents

Introduction

Finding quality informational texts at the appropriate level can be quite challenging. That's why we created this collection of compelling articles, which were originally printed in our award-winning classroom magazine *Scholastic News*. The passages have been carefully selected to engage students' interest and have been leveled to meet the needs of all readers. Each article comes in three Lexile levels. But because all versions of an article look alike, students need not know they're getting different levels. To identify the reading levels, simply look at the shape around the page numbers.

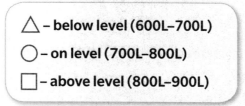

$\triangle$ – **below level (600L–700L)**

$\bigcirc$ – **on level (700L–800L)**

$\square$ – **above level (800L–900L)**

Each article comes with a variety of comprehension questions, including multiple choice, short response, and essay. These questions challenge students to identify the main idea and supporting details; make inferences; determine cause and effect; identify author's purpose and point of view; interpret maps, charts, and diagrams; build vocabulary; summarize; and more. In fact, you can use this book to help students get ready for standardized tests.

One way to build students' comprehension is to encourage them to mark up the text as they read—circling, underlining, or highlighting main ideas, supporting details, and key vocabulary words. This simple action helps them process what they're reading, making it easier to focus on important ideas and make connections. For more test-taking tips, photocopy and distribute the helpful hints below for students.

TEST-TAKING TIPS FOR STUDENTS:

- Make sure you understand each question fully before you answer it. Underline key words. Restate the question in your own words.

- Always refer to the text to find answers. It's a good idea to go back and reread parts of the text to answer a question.

- When you finish, check all your answers. You may find a mistake that you can correct.

- Most important, relax! Some people get nervous before a test. That's normal. Just do your best.

School on a Bus

1. For millions of kids in India, getting an education is a big challenge. But in some parts of the South Asian country, school buses have come to the rescue. The buses don't take kids to school, though. The buses are the schools!

2. Why are buses being used as schools? India's economy has improved greatly in recent years. But millions of people there still live in poverty. Many kids who live in poor areas can't get to schools that are far away. Other kids have to work to help support their families.

3. To help these children, the "classroom buses" run in cities such as Hyderabad, Mumbai, New Delhi, and Pune. Like regular school buses, they go around and pick up kids. Each bus has a teacher on

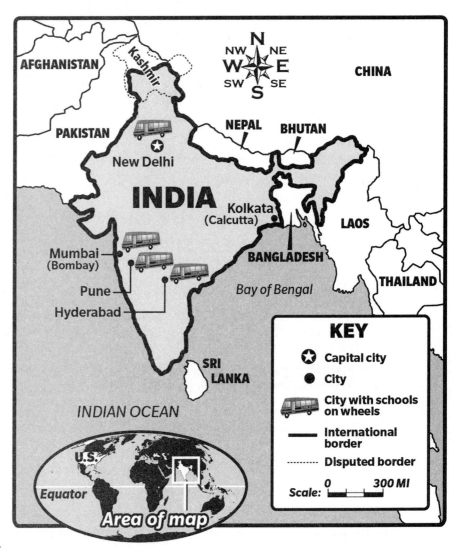

AFGHANISTAN
CHINA
Kashmir
PAKISTAN
NEPAL
BHUTAN
New Delhi
INDIA
Kolkata (Calcutta)
LAOS
Mumbai (Bombay)
BANGLADESH
THAILAND
Pune
Hyderabad
Bay of Bengal
SRI LANKA
INDIAN OCEAN

N NE NW NE W E SW SE S

KEY
⭐ Capital city
● City
🚌 City with schools on wheels
── International border
┈┈ Disputed border
Scale: 0 ──── 300 MI

U.S.
Equator
Area of map

A classroom bus in India

My School on Wheels

board. It also has a blackboard, shelves of books, crayons, and other supplies. When the buses park, the lessons begin. The kids range in age from 6 to 14. They are grouped by skill level. They learn reading, writing, math, and more.

4. Making education available to more people in India is no easy task. India is home to 1.2 billion people. More than one third are unable to read and write. But the schools on wheels are helping to give more kids opportunities—and hope for a better future.

Name: _____

Directions: Read the article "School on a Bus." Then answer the questions below.

1. **Which sentence best summarizes the second paragraph?**

    A. The classroom buses have all the same supplies as regular classrooms.

    B. Many kids in India live in poverty and are unable to attend school.

    c. Many people in India never learned to read or write.

    D. Many kids in India have to work to help support their families.

2. **Explain two ways that schools on buses help educate children. Use details from the passage to support your answer.**

    _____

    _____

    _____

3. **Match each word in Column A with the word in Column B that has the <u>opposite</u> meaning.**

Column A	Column B
available	wealth
recent	scarce
poverty	historic

4. **Which sentence best explains why the author thinks that the school buses have "come to the rescue"?**

    A. The buses allow many students who would not receive an education otherwise to go to school.

    B. India is a large country with many students who go to school.

    c. The school buses pick up students, then park before the lessons begin.

    D. The buses are helping transport students to better schools.

5. **Which feature on the map best helps your understanding of the article?**

    A. It shows international borders.

    B. It shows how far India is from the United States.

    c. It shows how close India is to the equator.

    D. It shows which areas have schools on wheels.

School on a Bus

1   For millions of kids in India, getting an education is a big challenge. But in some parts of the South Asian country, school buses have come to the rescue. The buses don't take kids to school, though. The buses are the schools!

2   Why are buses being used as schools? Even though India's economy has improved greatly in recent years, millions of people there still live in poverty. Many kids who live in poor areas can't get to schools that are far away. Other kids have to work to help support their families.

3   To help these children, the "classroom buses" run in cities such as Hyderabad, Mumbai, New Delhi, and Pune. Like regular school buses, they go around and pick up kids. Each bus has a teacher on board. It also

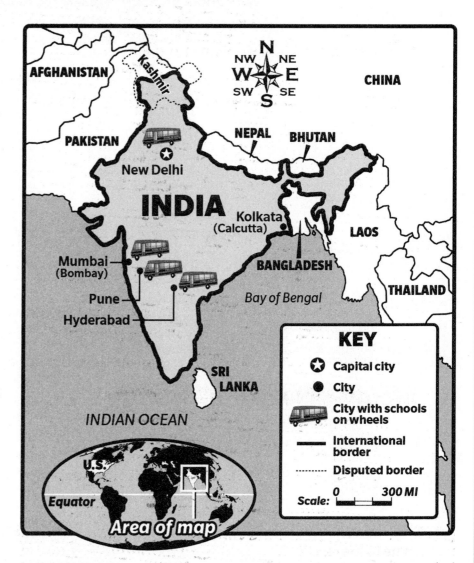

INDIA

AFGHANISTAN
Kashmir
PAKISTAN
New Delhi
CHINA
NEPAL
BHUTAN
Kolkata (Calcutta)
LAOS
Mumbai (Bombay)
Pune
Hyderabad
BANGLADESH
Bay of Bengal
THAILAND
SRI LANKA
INDIAN OCEAN

KEY
⭐ Capital city
● City
🚌 City with schools on wheels
—— International border
------ Disputed border
Scale: 0 — 300 MI

U.S.
Equator
Area of map

A classroom bus in India

My School on Wheels

has a blackboard, shelves of books, crayons, and other supplies. When the buses park, the lessons begin. The kids range in age from 6 to 14 and are grouped by skill level. They learn reading, writing, math, and more.

4   Making education available to more people in India is no easy task. India is home to 1.2 billion people. More than one third are unable to read and write. But the schools on wheels are helping to give more kids opportunities—and hope for a better future.

Name: _____

Directions: Read the article "School on a Bus." Then answer the questions below.

1. **Which sentence best summarizes the second paragraph?**

   A. The classroom buses have all the same supplies as regular classrooms.

   B. Many kids in India have to work to help support their families.

   C. Many people in India never learned to read or write.

   D. Many kids in India live in poverty and are unable to attend school.

2. **Explain two ways that schools on buses help educate children. Use details from the passage to support your answer.**

   _____

   _____

   _____

3. **Match each word in Column A with the word in Column B that has the <u>opposite</u> meaning.**

Column A	Column B
poverty	historic
recent	scarce
available	wealth

4. **Which sentence best explains why the author thinks that the school buses have "come to the rescue"?**

   A. India is a large country with many students who go to school.

   B. The buses allow many students who would not receive an education otherwise to go to school.

   C. The buses are helping transport students to better schools.

   D. The school buses pick up students, then park before the lessons begin.

5. **Which feature on the map best helps your understanding of the article?**

   A. It shows how far India is from the United States.

   B. It shows how close India is to the equator.

   C. It shows which areas have schools on wheels.

   D. It shows international borders.

School on a Bus

1 For millions of kids in India, getting an education is a big challenge. But in some parts of the South Asian country, school buses have come to the rescue. The buses don't take kids to school, though. The buses are the schools!

2 Why are buses being used as schools? Although India's economy has improved greatly in recent years, millions of people there still live in poverty. Many kids who live in poor areas can't get to schools that are far away. Other kids have to work to help support their families.

3 To help these children, the "classroom buses" operate in cities such as Hyderabad, Mumbai, New Delhi, and Pune. Like regular school buses, they go around and pick up kids. Each bus has a teacher on board, along

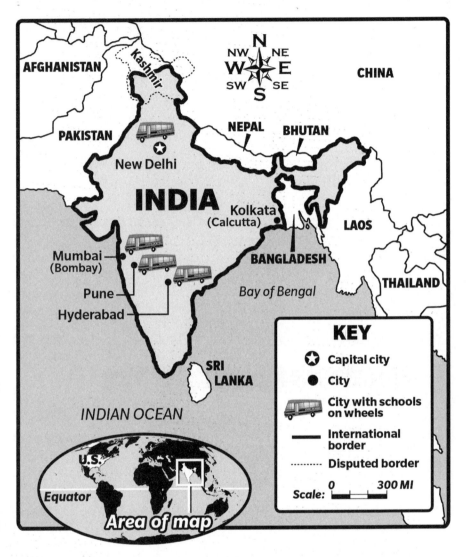

with a blackboard, shelves of books, crayons, and other supplies. When the buses park, the lessons begin. The kids range in age from 6 to 14. Grouped by skill level, they learn reading, writing, math, and more.

4 Making education available to more people in India is no easy task. India is home to 1.2 billion people. More than one third are unable to read and write. But the schools on wheels are helping to give more kids opportunities—and hope for a better future.

A classroom bus in India

My School on Wheels

Name: _____

Directions: Read the article "School on a Bus." Then answer the questions below.

1. Which sentence best summarizes the second paragraph?

A. Many kids in India live in poverty and are unable to attend school.

B. The classroom buses have all the same supplies as regular classrooms.

C. Many kids in India have to work to help support their families.

D. Many people in India never learned to read or write.

2. Explain two ways that schools on buses help educate children. Use details from the passage to support your answer.

_____

_____

_____

3. Match each word in Column A with the word in Column B that has the <u>opposite</u> meaning.

Column A	Column B
recent	scarce
poverty	historic
available	wealth

4. Which sentence best explains why the author thinks that the school buses have "come to the rescue"?

A. India is a large country with many students who go to school.

B. The school buses pick up students, then park before the lessons begin.

C. The buses allow many students who would not receive an education otherwise to go to school.

D. The buses are helping transport students to better schools.

5. Which feature on the map best helps your understanding of the article?

A. It shows which areas have schools on wheels.

B. It shows how far India is from the United States.

C. It shows how close India is to the equator.

D. It shows international borders.

A Dynamic Duo

1   It was the fourth quarter of a football game between Army and Rutgers University. The score was tied. Rutgers player Eric LeGrand went to make a tackle. He collided with another player. When Eric fell to the ground, he couldn't move. He was **paralyzed** from the neck down.

2   For the past several years, Eric has worked with a team of physical therapists. They're trying to help him move again. One member of his team has been especially helpful—a black Labrador retriever mix named Willie.

3   Willie is a service dog. She is trained to work with patients at the Kessler Rehabilitation Center in New Jersey. She belongs to one of Eric's physical therapists, Sandra Wojciehowski (who-juh-HOW-skee). Willie helps Eric and other patients build muscle. The playful pup also helps stressed-out patients feel better.

A History of Helping

4   Dogs are very loyal and obedient. They have sharp senses of smell and hearing. Long ago, people realized these qualities could help people with disabilities.

5   After World War I, service dogs guided soldiers who had lost their sight. In the 1960s, people began training dogs to help people with other disabilities. Today, tens of thousands of service dogs perform many jobs across the country.

Eric LeGrand with Willie the service dog

A service dog is specially trained to help its disabled owner.

Working Out

6   Willie helps Eric with his exercises. In the beginning, Eric worked out at Kessler for three hours a day, three days a week. Therapy is hard. But Willie is always there to lighten the mood. She also prods Eric when needed.

7   In one exercise, Eric sits up on a table. Sandra gives Willie a command to push. The dog nudges Eric's back with her nose. Eric uses his back muscles to keep from falling over.

8   Doctors never expected Eric to be able to do these kinds of exercises. After the accident, he couldn't breathe on his own or eat. He couldn't move any part of his body except his head.

9   But Eric has worked hard to get better. He can now move muscles in his shoulders and back. He can feel throughout his body. Doctors say he has made remarkable progress.

10   Eric's recovery would have been much harder without Willie. "Even though you're working, you can have a good time doing it," he says. "So that definitely helps."

11   When he finishes an exercise, Eric usually lies back on the table. He's tired from his workout. Willie curls up next to him. She puts her head on his chest. Often, Eric will ask to pet Willie. Sandra then takes his hand and uses it to scratch Willie's ears and belly. Eric hopes that someday he'll be able to pet Willie on his own.

Name: _____

Directions: Read the article "A Dynamic Duo." Then answer the questions below.

1. Which statement best helps the reader understand the meaning of *paralyzed*?

    A. Rutgers player Eric LeGrand went to make a tackle. *(paragraph 1)*

    B. . . . Eric has worked with a team of physical therapists. *(paragraph 2)*

    C. When Eric fell to the ground, he couldn't move. *(paragraph 1)*

    D. Willie helps Eric and other patients build muscle. *(paragraph 3)*

2. After World War I, service dogs were trained to _____.

    A. guide soldiers who had lost their eyesight during the war

    B. guide children who had been born blind

    C. comfort people who were paralyzed

    D. help patients with physical therapy

3. What is the section "Working Out" mostly about?

    A. Eric doesn't like physical therapy.

    B. With Willie's help, Eric has made a lot of progress in regaining his strength.

    C. Working with Willie often tires Eric out.

    D. Eric hopes to pet Willie on his own one day.

4. Which of the following details best supports the answer to question 3?

    A. [Willie] is trained to work with patients at the Kessler Rehabilitation Center in New Jersey. *(paragraph 3)*

    B. In the beginning, Eric worked out at Kessler for three hours a day, three days a week. *(paragraph 6)*

    C. Doctors never expected Eric to be able to do these kinds of exercises. *(paragraph 8)*

    D. When he finishes an exercise, Eric usually lies back on the table. *(paragraph 11)*

5. Which sentence best summarizes the article?

    A. Dogs can be trained to do all sorts of jobs for people, including aiding people with disabilities.

    B. Dogs are loyal, obedient, and helpful to people.

    C. Eric LeGrand works hard to get his body moving again after a collision with another player left him paralyzed.

    D. A service dog named Willie is helping a football player recover from his severe injuries.

A Dynamic Duo

1   It was the fourth quarter of a football game between Army and Rutgers University. The score was tied. Rutgers player Eric LeGrand went to make a tackle. But after he collided with another player, Eric lay motionless on the field. He was paralyzed from the neck down.

2   For the past several years, Eric has worked with a team of physical therapists. Their goal is to get movement back in the rest of his body. Doctors say he has made remarkable progress. One member of his **rehabilitation** team has been a special inspiration—a black Labrador retriever mix named Willie.

3   Willie is a service dog. She is trained to work with patients at the Kessler Rehabilitation Center in New Jersey. She belongs to one of Eric's physical therapists, Sandra Wojciehowski (who-juh-HOW-skee).

Willie helps Eric and other patients build muscle strength and regain their balance. The playful pup also comforts people who are stressed from being severely injured.

A History of Helping

4   Dogs are called "man's best friend" for good reasons. They're extremely loyal and obedient. They also have keen senses of smell and hearing. In the 1920s, people realized these qualities could help people with disabilities.

5   The first modern service dogs guided soldiers who had lost their sight during World War I. In the 1960s, people began training dogs to help people with other disabilities. Today, tens of thousands of service dogs perform many jobs across the country.

Eric LeGrand with Willie the service dog

A service dog is specially trained to help its disabled owner.

Working Out

6   In the beginning, Eric worked out at Kessler for three hours a day, three days a week. The therapy is difficult. But Willie is always there to lighten the mood. She also prods Eric when needed.

7   In one exercise, Eric sits up on a table. When Sandra gives Willie a command to push, the dog nudges Eric's back with her nose. As Willie pushes him forward, Eric uses his back muscles to keep from falling over.

8   Doctors never expected Eric to be able to do these kinds of exercises. When he was first injured, he couldn't breathe on his own or eat. He couldn't move any part of his body but his head. Doctors weren't sure if he would ever move again.

9   But Eric has worked hard to get better. He can now move muscles in his shoulders and back. He has sensation throughout his body.

10   Eric's recovery would have been much harder without Willie. "Even though you're working, you can have a good time doing it," he says. "So that definitely helps."

11   When he finishes an exercise, Eric usually lies back on the table. He's tired from his workout. Willie curls up next to him with her head on his chest. Often, Eric will ask to pet Willie. Sandra then takes his hand and uses it to scratch Willie's ears and belly. Eric hopes that someday he'll be able to pet Willie on his own.

Name: _____

Directions: Read the article "A Dynamic Duo." Then answer the questions below.

1. Which statement best helps the reader understand the meaning of *rehabilitation*?

  A. Their goal is to get movement back in the rest of his body. *(paragraph 2)*

  B. Today, tens of thousands of service dogs perform many jobs across the country. *(paragraph 5)*

  C. Rutgers player Eric LeGrand went to make a tackle. *(paragraph 1)*

  D. [Dogs] also have keen senses of smell and hearing. *(paragraph 4)*

2. The first modern service dogs were trained to _____.

  A. help patients with physical therapy

  B. guide soldiers who had lost their eyesight during World War I

  C. comfort people who were paralyzed

  D. guide soldiers who had been born blind

3. What is the section "Working Out" mostly about?

  A. With Willie's help, Eric has made a lot of progress in regaining his strength.

  B. Eric doesn't like physical therapy.

  C. Working with Willie often tires Eric out.

  D. Eric hopes to pet Willie on his own one day.

4. Which of the following details best supports the answer to question 3?

  A. When he finishes an exercise, Eric usually lies back on the table. *(paragraph 11)*

  B. [Willie] is trained to work with patients at the Kessler Rehabilitation Center in New Jersey. *(paragraph 3)*

  C. In the beginning, Eric worked out at Kessler for three hours a day, three days a week. *(paragraph 6)*

  D. Doctors never expected Eric to be able to do these kinds of exercises. *(paragraph 8)*

5. Which sentence best summarizes the article?

  A. Eric LeGrand is working hard to rehabilitate his body after a collision with another player left him paralyzed.

  B. A service dog named Willie is helping a football player recover from his severe injuries.

  C. Dogs are called "man's best friend" because they are loyal, obedient, and helpful to people.

  D. Dogs can be trained to do all sorts of jobs for people, including aiding people with disabilities.

A Dynamic Duo

1   It was the fourth quarter of a football game between Army and Rutgers University. The score was tied. Rutgers player Eric LeGrand went to make a tackle, something he had done so many times before. But after he collided with another player, Eric lay motionless on the field. He had suffered a spinal injury. He was paralyzed from the neck down.

2   For the past several years, Eric has worked with a team of physical therapists to try to get movement back in the rest of his body. Doctors say he has made remarkable progress. One member of his **rehabilitation** team has been a special inspiration—a black Labrador retriever mix named Willie.

3   Willie is a service dog trained to work with patients at the Kessler Rehabilitation Center in New Jersey. She belongs to one of Eric's physical therapists, Sandra Wojciehowski (who-juh-HOW-skee). Willie helps Eric and other patients build muscle strength and regain their balance. The playful pup also provides much-needed comfort to people who are dealing with the emotional stress of being severely injured.

A History of Helping

4   Dogs are called "man's best friend" for good reasons. They're extremely loyal and obedient. They also have keen senses of smell and hearing. In the 1920s, people began to realize that these qualities could help people with disabilities.

5   The first modern service dogs were trained to guide soldiers who had lost their

Eric LeGrand
with Willie the
service dog

A service dog is specially trained to help its disabled owner.

sight during World War I (1914–1918). In the 1960s, people began training dogs to aid people with other disabilities. Today, tens of thousands of service dogs perform many jobs across the country.

Working Out

6   In the beginning, Eric worked out at Kessler for three hours a day, three days a week. The therapy is difficult, but Willie is always there to lighten the mood. She also prods Eric when needed.

7   In one exercise, Eric sits upright on a table. When Sandra gives Willie a command to push, the dog nudges Eric's back with her nose. As Willie pushes him forward, Eric uses the muscles in his back to keep him from falling over.

8   Doctors never expected Eric to be able to do these kinds of exercises. When he was first injured, he couldn't breathe on his own, eat, or move any part of his body but his head. Doctors weren't sure he would ever move again.

9   But Eric has worked tirelessly at his recovery. He can now move muscles in his shoulders and back. He has sensation throughout his body.

10   Eric's recovery would have been much harder without Willie. "Even though you're working, you can have a good time doing it," he says. "So that definitely helps."

11   When he finishes an exercise, Eric usually lies back on the table, tired from his workout. Willie curls up next to him with her head on his chest. Often, Eric will ask to pet Willie. Sandra then takes his hand and uses it to scratch Willie's ears and belly. Eric hopes that someday he'll be able to pet Willie on his own.

Name: _____

Directions: Read the article "A Dynamic Duo." Then answer the questions below.

1. Which statement best helps the reader understand the meaning of *rehabilitation*?

    A. Rutgers player Eric LeGrand went to make a tackle, something he had done so many times before. *(paragraph 1)*

    B. . . . Eric has worked with a team of physical therapists to try to get movement back in the rest of his body. *(paragraph 2)*

    C. [Dogs] also have keen senses of smell and hearing. *(paragraph 4)*

    D. Today, tens of thousands of service dogs perform many jobs across the country. *(paragraph 5)*

2. The first modern service dogs were trained to _____.

    A. help patients with physical therapy

    B. comfort people who were paralyzed

    C. guide soldiers who had lost their eyesight during World War I

    D. guide young children who had been born blind

3. What is the section "Working Out" mostly about?

    A. Eric doesn't like physical therapy.

    B. Working with Willie often tires Eric out.

    C. Eric hopes to pet Willie on his own one day.

    D. With Willie's help, Eric has made a lot of progress in regaining his strength.

4. Which of the following details best supports the answer to question 3?

    A. Doctors never expected Eric to be able to do these kinds of exercises. *(paragraph 8)*

    B. When he finishes an exercise, Eric usually lies back on the table . . . *(paragraph 11)*

    C. Willie is a service dog trained to work with patients at the Kessler Rehabilitation Center in New Jersey. *(paragraph 3)*

    D. In the beginning, Eric worked out at Kessler for three hours a day, three days a week. *(paragraph 6)*

5. Which sentence best summarizes the article?

    A. Dogs are called "man's best friend" because they are loyal, obedient, and helpful to people.

    B. Dogs can be trained to do all sorts of jobs for people, including aiding people with disabilities.

    C. A service dog named Willie is helping a football player recover from his severe injuries.

    D. Eric LeGrand is working hard to rehabilitate his body after a collision with another player left him paralyzed.

Don't Just Stand By

1   Nathalie Vazquez was first bullied in third grade. The bully's name was Katie.* She would boss Nathalie around. Katie also spread hurtful rumors about her at school.

2   This continued for years. In seventh grade, Katie's bullying got physical. One day she pushed Nathalie into a trash can. Nathalie was frustrated. Many of her classmates just stood by and watched.

3   "I felt really upset because I didn't have any backup," says Nathalie, who lives in California. "I didn't have anyone who would help me. I was really alone."

4   Does Nathalie's story sound familiar? Studies show that about one out of three kids is bullied at school. Bullying includes hitting, name-calling, and rejecting kids on purpose. It also includes cyberbullying. That's when someone uses the internet to send mean messages or spread rumors.

Innocent Bystanders?

5   Bullying isn't just about the victim and the bully. The people who witness bullying often play an important role.

6   When these bystanders keep quiet, they send the message that a bully's actions are OK. But it doesn't have to be that way. Bystanders actually have more power than they realize.

7   "Research shows that just by stepping in and saying, 'Hey, that's not OK, don't do that,' the bullying stops in at least half of the cases," says Kim Storey. She's a bully-prevention expert.

Bullying comes in different forms.

Standing Up

8   Kids who see other kids getting bullied may be afraid to step in. It can be risky, especially when a bully is beating up another kid. Experts say kids don't have to go that far. Bystanders can often help with smaller acts.

9   For Nathalie, a classmate's small act went a long way. In seventh grade, a student told Katie to leave Nathalie alone. "It felt really good," says Nathalie. "It really helps a lot. If there's one person who stands up, [others] are going to start to do something too."

Raising Awareness

10   After that, Nathalie felt more confident. She was able to speak up about her bullying experiences. Later that year, she started an organization. She called it "No-to-Hate! Stop Bullying." It teaches others about bullying and how to stand up to it.

11   Nathalie's organization worked with officials at her school. Together, they hosted events that teach students about bullying.

12   "We want to raise awareness to stop bullying," said Nathalie. "We want [bullying victims] to speak up and defend their rights. No one deserves to feel or be treated that way."

* Name has been changed to protect the student's privacy.

Name: _____

Directions: Read the article "Don't Just Stand By." Then answer the questions below.

1. What is the author's purpose?

   A. To entertain readers with a story about kids who stood up to bullies

   B. To inform readers about cyberbullying

   C. To educate readers about the role of bystanders in bullying situations

   D. To persuade readers to talk about bullying and start organizations that help prevent it

2. Which sentence from the article best supports the answer to question 1?

   A. Bystanders can often help with smaller acts. *(paragraph 8)*

   B. In seventh grade, Katie's bullying got physical. *(paragraph 2)*

   C. That's when someone uses the internet to send mean messages or spread rumors. *(paragraph 4)*

   D. "No one deserves to feel or be treated that way." *(paragraph 12)*

3. Which best describes the main idea of the section "Innocent Bystanders?"

   A. Bullying is not OK, no matter what.

   B. Bystanders are often the ones to blame for bullying.

   C. Bullying will always stop if bystanders step in.

   D. Bystanders' actions can have an effect on bullies' actions.

4. Which conclusion can be drawn about Nathalie's organization, "No-to-Hate! Stop Bullying"?

   A. Bullying is no longer a problem at Nathalie's school, thanks to the organization.

   B. Nathalie's experiences with bullying gave her the idea for the organization.

   C. School leaders have not supported the work of the organization.

   D. The organization has received more attention than Nathalie expected.

5. Read this sentence from paragraph 4.

   Studies show that about one out of three kids is bullied at school.

   What is the most likely reason that the author included this detail?

   A. To show that bullying affects many kids, not just Nathalie

   B. To compare bullying at school with bullying in other places

   C. To prove that bullying is not as serious a problem as it seems

   D. To support the idea that bystanders can help stop bullying

6. The article focuses on Nathalie's experience with bullying. On another sheet of paper, describe the problem she faced and how it was resolved. Use details from the article in your response.

Don't Just Stand By

1   For Nathalie Vazquez, the bullying started when she was in third grade. The bully, Katie,* would boss Nathalie around. She would spread hurtful rumors about Nathalie at school.

2   This continued for years. By seventh grade, Katie's bullying had gotten physical. One day, she grabbed Nathalie and pushed her into a trash can in front of other students. Nathalie felt frustrated. So many of her classmates just stood by and watched her being bullied.

3   "I felt really upset because I didn't have any backup," says Nathalie, who lives in Chula Vista, California. "I didn't have anyone who would help me. I was really alone."

4   Do Nathalie's experiences seem familiar? Studies show that about one out of three kids is bullied at school. Bullying includes everything from hitting and name-calling to excluding kids on purpose. It also includes cyberbullying. That's when someone uses the internet to send mean messages or spread rumors.

Innocent Bystanders?

5   Bullying isn't about just the victim and the bully. The people who witness bullying often play an important role. Experts say these bystanders can actually make a bullying situation worse.

6   "If you just stand by and don't say anything, the victim doesn't realize that they have any support," says Kim Storey. She's a bullying-prevention expert.

7   Experts say that by keeping quiet, bystanders send the message that a bully's actions are OK. But that doesn't have to be the case. Bystanders actually have more power than they may realize.

8   "Research shows that just by stepping in and saying, 'Hey, that's not OK, don't do that,' the bullying stops in at least half of the cases," says Storey.

Bullying comes in different forms.

Standing Up

9   Kids who see other kids getting bullied at school may be afraid to get involved. Stepping in when a bully is beating up another kid can be risky. Experts say kids don't have to go that far—especially if they don't feel safe. Bystanders can often help with smaller acts.

10   For Nathalie, those kinds of actions went a long way. In seventh grade, a classmate stood up to Katie and told her to leave Nathalie alone. "It felt really good," says Nathalie. "It really helps a lot, because if there's one person who stands up, [others] are going to start to do something too."

Raising Awareness

11   After her classmate finally stood up for Nathalie, she gained the confidence to speak up about her bullying experiences. Later that year, she started an organization to help educate others about bullying and how to stand up to it. She named it "No-to-Hate! Stop Bullying."

12   Nathalie's organization has worked with officials at her school. Together, they've hosted assemblies and other events that teach students about bullying.

13   "We want to raise awareness to stop bullying," said Nathalie. "We want [bullying victims] to speak up and defend their rights. No one deserves to feel or be treated that way."

* Name has been changed to protect the student's privacy.

Name: _____

Directions: Read the article "Don't Just Stand By." Then answer the questions below.

1. What is the author's purpose?

A. To inform readers about cyberbullying

B. To educate readers about the role of bystanders in bullying situations

C. To persuade readers to talk about bullying and start organizations that help prevent it

D. To entertain readers with a story about kids who stood up to bullies

2. Which sentence from the article best supports the answer to question 1?

A. "No one deserves to feel or be treated that way." *(paragraph 13)*

B. That's when someone uses the internet to send mean messages or spread rumors. *(paragraph 4)*

C. By seventh grade, Katie's bullying had gotten physical. *(paragraph 2)*

D. Bystanders can often help with smaller acts. *(paragraph 9)*

3. Which best describes the main idea of the section "Innocent Bystanders?"

A. Bystanders' actions can have an effect on bullies' actions.

B. Bullying will always stop if bystanders step in.

C. Bullying is not OK, no matter what.

D. Bystanders are often the ones to blame for bullying.

4. Which conclusion can be drawn about Nathalie's organization, "No-to-Hate! Stop Bullying"?

A. Bullying is no longer a problem at Nathalie's school, thanks to the organization.

B. School leaders have not supported the work of the organization.

C. Nathalie's experiences with bullying gave her the idea for the organization.

D. The organization has received more attention than Nathalie expected.

5. Read this sentence from paragraph 4.

Studies show that about one out of three kids is bullied at school.

What is the most likely reason that the author included this detail?

A. To support the idea that bystanders can help stop bullying

B. To prove that bullying is not as serious a problem as it seems

C. To show that bullying affects many kids, not just Nathalie

D. To compare bullying at school with bullying in other places

6. The article focuses on Nathalie's experience with bullying. On a separate sheet of paper, describe the problem she faced and how it was resolved. Use details from the article in your response.

Don't Just Stand By

1   For Nathalie Vazquez, the bullying started when she was in third grade. The bully, Katie,* would boss Nathalie around and spread hurtful rumors about her at school.

2   This continued for years. By seventh grade, Katie's bullying had gotten physical. One day, she grabbed Nathalie and pushed her into a trash can in front of other students. Nathalie was frustrated because so many of her classmates often stood by and watched her being bullied.

3   "I felt really upset because I didn't have any backup," says Nathalie, who lives in Chula Vista, California. "I didn't have anyone who would help me. I was really alone."

4   Do Nathalie's experiences seem familiar? Studies show that about one out of every three kids is bullied at school. Bullying includes everything from hitting and name-calling to excluding kids on purpose. It also includes cyberbullying. That's when someone uses the internet to send mean messages or spread rumors.

Innocent Bystanders?

5   As Nathalie knows, bullying isn't about just the victim and the bully. Bystanders, the people who witness bullying, often play an important role. Experts say bystanders can actually make a bullying situation worse.

6   "If you just stand by and don't say anything, the victim doesn't realize that they have any support," says Kim Storey. She's a bullying-prevention expert.

7   Experts say that by keeping quiet, bystanders send the message that a bully's actions are OK. But that doesn't have to be the case. Bystanders actually have more power than they may realize.

8   "Research shows that just by stepping in and saying, 'Hey, that's not OK, don't do that,' the bullying stops in at least half of the cases," says Storey.

Bullying comes in different forms.

Standing Up

9   Kids who see other kids getting bullied at school may be afraid to get involved. Stepping in when a bully is beating up another kid can be risky. Experts say kids don't have to go that far—especially if they don't feel safe. Bystanders can often help with smaller acts.

10   For Nathalie, those kinds of actions went a long way. In seventh grade, a classmate stood up to Katie and told her to leave Nathalie alone. "It felt really good," says Nathalie. "It really helps a lot, because if there's one person who stands up, [others] are going to start to do something too."

Raising Awareness

11   After her classmate finally stood up for Nathalie, she gained the confidence to speak up about her bullying experiences. Later that year, she started an organization to help educate others about bullying and how to stand up to it. She named it "No-to-Hate! Stop Bullying."

12   Nathalie's organization has worked with officials at her school. Together, they've hosted assemblies and other events that teach students about bullying.

13   "We want to raise awareness to stop bullying," said Nathalie. "We want [bullying victims] to speak up and defend their rights. No one deserves to feel or be treated that way."

* Name has been changed to protect the student's privacy.

Name: _____

Directions: Read the article "Don't Just Stand By." Then answer the questions below.

1. What is the author's purpose?

 A. To educate readers about the role of bystanders in bullying situations

 B. To inform readers about cyberbullying

 C. To persuade readers to talk about bullying and start organizations that help prevent it

 D. To entertain readers with a story about kids who stood up to bullies

2. Which sentence from the article best supports the answer to question 1?

 A. That's when someone uses the internet to send mean messages or spread rumors. *(paragraph 4)*

 B. Bystanders can often help with smaller acts. *(paragraph 9)*

 C. By seventh grade, Katie's bullying had gotten physical. *(paragraph 2)*

 D. "No one deserves to feel or be treated that way." *(paragraph 13)*

3. Which best describes the main idea of the section "Innocent Bystanders?"

 A. Bystanders are often the ones to blame for bullying.

 B. Bullying is not OK, no matter what.

 C. Bystanders' actions can have an effect on bullies' actions.

 D. Bullying will always stop if bystanders step in.

4. Which conclusion can be drawn about Nathalie's organization, "No-to-Hate! Stop Bullying"?

 A. Nathalie's experiences with bullying gave her the idea for the organization.

 B. Bullying is no longer a problem at Nathalie's school, thanks to the organization.

 C. School leaders have not supported the work of the organization.

 D. The organization has received more attention than Nathalie expected.

5. Read this sentence from paragraph 4.

 Studies show that about one out of every three kids is bullied at school.

 What is the most likely reason that the author included this detail?

 A. To prove that bullying is not as serious a problem as it seems

 B. To show that bullying affects many kids, not just Nathalie

 C. To support the idea that bystanders can help stop bullying

 D. To compare bullying at school with bullying in other places

6. The article focuses on Nathalie's experience with bullying. On a separate sheet of paper, describe the problem she faced and how it was resolved. Use details from the article in your response.

For Sale: Volcanic Power

1   What do you think of when you hear the name *Iceland*? Many people think of ice and snow. But the island nation of Iceland is made up of more than 30 active volcanoes. That means there's plenty of heat below its surface.

2   People in Iceland use this heat to make electricity. That energy is used in homes and businesses. Energy produced this way is called geothermal power.

3   Iceland has only about 317,000 people. So it uses just a small part of that energy. Iceland's government wants to sell the unused energy to its neighbors across the ocean. The problem is how to get it there.

4   Engineers suggested building a long undersea cable. The cable would connect the island of Iceland with the rest of Europe. It would stretch nearly 1,000 miles. It would be the world's longest power cord.

Endless Energy

5   Iceland formed about 70 million years ago. Molten rock rose from the ocean floor. When it cooled, it formed the island of Iceland. The islands of Hawaii formed in a similar way.

6   Today, rivers of magma still boil under Iceland's surface. A volcano erupts there about every three years.

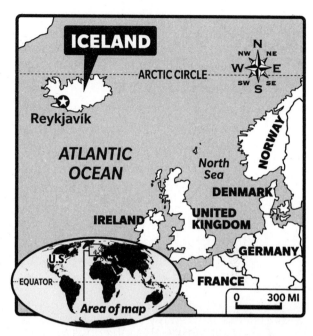

A geothermal plant next to a hot spring

7   Iceland's underground volcanic activity also creates pools of steam water. These are called hot springs. The steam from these hot springs is used to create geothermal energy.

8   Geothermal power is a renewable resource. That means it can never be used up. That's because the supply of heat from within Earth is endless. Using renewable energy is cleaner than burning coal or natural gas. That's how the United States and many other countries make electricity. Burning those fuels creates pollution.

Making a Connection

9   Many countries in Europe want to switch to geothermal power. The proposed undersea cable would first link Iceland to the United Kingdom. Then it would link Iceland to the rest of Europe. That's about 1,200 miles away.

10   This electrical cable has been discussed for many years. But officials in Europe had thought it would be too expensive. Now, European countries are willing to pay more for renewable energy to protect the environment.

Name: _____

Directions: Read the article "For Sale: Volcanic Power." Then answer the questions below.

1. Which detail is most important to include in a summary of the article?

A. But the island nation of Iceland is made up of more than 30 active volcanoes. *(paragraph 1)*

B. The islands of Hawaii formed in a similar way. *(paragraph 5)*

C. Iceland's government wants to sell the unused energy to its neighbors across the ocean. *(paragraph 3)*

D. A volcano erupts there about every three years. *(paragraph 6)*

2. How does the map add to the reader's understanding of the article's main idea?

A. It shows the distance between Iceland and the rest of Europe.

B. It shows where the capital of Iceland is located.

C. It shows that Iceland is an island with active volcanoes.

D. It shows the size of Iceland compared with that of other European countries.

3. Which detail from the passage best supports the answer to question 2?

A. Iceland formed about 70 million years ago. *(paragraph 5)*

B. But the island nation of Iceland is made up of more than 30 active volcanoes. *(paragraph 1)*

C. Now, European countries are willing to pay more for renewable energy to protect the environment. *(paragraph 10)*

D. Then [the cable] would link Iceland to the rest of Europe. That's about 1,200 miles away. *(paragraph 9)*

4. On the chart, describe one cause and one effect of geothermal energy produced in Iceland.

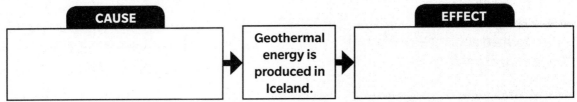

CAUSE		EFFECT
	Geothermal energy is produced in Iceland.	

5. How does the author support the idea that Iceland produces more energy than it uses?

A. By comparing sources of energy used in the U.S. with those used in Iceland

B. By stating the population of Iceland

C. By describing how Iceland formed

D. By explaining what a renewable resource is

6. Based on the article, which conclusion can be drawn about Iceland?

A. It has enough energy to sell to mainland Europe for many years to come.

B. Its government prefers not to deal with other countries.

C. It consumes more energy than most countries.

D. It produces a lot of pollution through its geothermal power plants.

For Sale: Volcanic Power

1   In the United States and many other countries, most electricity is created by burning coal or natural gas. But in Iceland, people get power from an unusual source. They use the heat from volcanoes!

2   When you hear the name *Iceland*, you may think of ice and snow. But this island nation is made up of more than 30 active volcanoes. And where there are active volcanoes, there's plenty of heat below Earth's surface. Power plants in Iceland turn heat from those volcanoes into electricity. That energy is used in homes and businesses. Energy produced this way is called geothermal power.

3   Because Iceland has only about 317,000 people, it uses just a small part of that energy. Iceland's government wants to sell the unused energy to its neighbors across the Atlantic. The problem is how to get it there.

4   Engineers have proposed building a long undersea cable. The cable would connect the island of Iceland with the rest of Europe. It would stretch nearly 1,000 miles. It would basically be the world's longest power cord.

Endless Energy

5   Iceland formed about 70 million years ago. Molten rock rose from the ocean floor and cooled to form this island. The islands of Hawaii formed in a similar way.

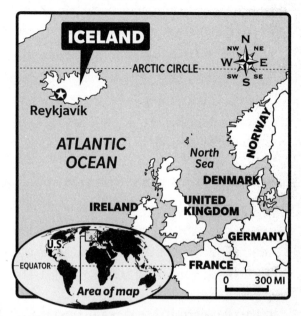

A geothermal plant next to a hot spring

6   Today, rivers of magma still boil under Iceland's surface. A major volcanic eruption happens there about every three years.

7   Iceland's underground volcanic activity also creates hot springs—pools of steam water. The steam from these hot springs is used to create geothermal energy.

8   Geothermal power is a renewable resource. That means it can never be used up. That's because the supply of heat from within Earth is endless. Using renewable energy is cleaner than burning coal or natural gas, which creates pollution.

Making a Connection

9   Many countries in Europe want to switch to geothermal power. The proposed undersea cable would first link Iceland to the United Kingdom. Then the cable would link Iceland to the rest of Europe. That's about 1,200 miles away.

10   The idea for an electrical cable connecting Iceland to Europe has been discussed for years. But officials in Europe had thought it would be too expensive. Now, European countries are willing to pay more for renewable energy to protect the environment.

Name: _____

Directions: Read the article "For Sale: Volcanic Power." Then answer the questions below.

1. Which detail is most important to include in a summary of the article?

    A. A major volcanic eruption happens there about every three years. *(paragraph 6)*

    B. When you hear the name *Iceland,* you may think of ice and snow. *(paragraph 2)*

    c. The islands of Hawaii formed in a similar way. *(paragraph 5)*

    D. Iceland's government wants to sell the unused energy to its neighbors across the Atlantic. *(paragraph 3)*

2. How does the map add to the reader's understanding of the article's main idea?

    A. It shows that Iceland is an island with active volcanoes.

    B. It shows the distance between Iceland and the rest of Europe.

    c. It shows where the capital of Iceland is located.

    D. It shows the size of Iceland compared with that of other European countries.

3. Which detail from the passage best supports the answer to question 2?

    A. Then the cable would link Iceland to the rest of Europe. That's about 1,200 miles away. *(paragraph 9)*

    B. But this island nation is made up of more than 30 active volcanoes. *(paragraph 2)*

    c. Molten rock rose from the ocean floor and cooled to form this island. *(paragraph 5)*

    D. Now, European countries are willing to pay more for renewable energy to protect the environment. *(paragraph 10)*

4. On the chart, describe one cause and one effect of geothermal energy produced in Iceland.

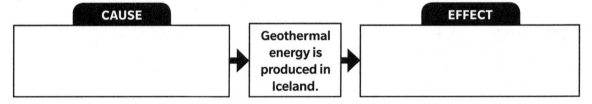

CAUSE		EFFECT
	Geothermal energy is produced in Iceland.	

5. How does the author support the idea that Iceland produces more energy than it uses?

    A. By explaining what a renewable resource is

    B. By describing how Iceland formed

    c. By comparing sources of energy used in the U.S. with those used in Iceland

    D. By stating the population of Iceland

6. Based on the article, which conclusion can be drawn about Iceland?

    A. Its government prefers not to deal with other countries.

    B. It consumes more energy than most countries.

    c. It has enough energy to sell to mainland Europe for many years to come.

    D. It produces a lot of pollution through its geothermal power plants.

For Sale: Volcanic Power

1   In the United States and many other countries, most electricity is created by burning coal or natural gas. But in Iceland, people get power from an unusual source. They use the heat from volcanoes!

2   When you hear the name *Iceland*, you may think of ice and snow. But this island nation is made up of more than 30 active volcanoes. And where there are active volcanoes, there's plenty of heat below Earth's surface. Power plants in Iceland turn heat from those volcanoes into electricity. That energy is used in homes and businesses. Energy produced this way is called geothermal power.

3   Because Iceland has only about 317,000 people, it uses just a small part of that energy. Iceland's government wants to sell the unused energy to its neighbors across the Atlantic. The problem is how to get it there.

4   Engineers have proposed building a long undersea cable to connect the island of Iceland with the rest of Europe. The cable would stretch nearly 1,000 miles. It would basically be the world's longest power cord.

Endless Energy

5   Iceland formed when molten rock gushed from the ocean floor and cooled about 70 million years ago. The islands of Hawaii formed in a similar way.

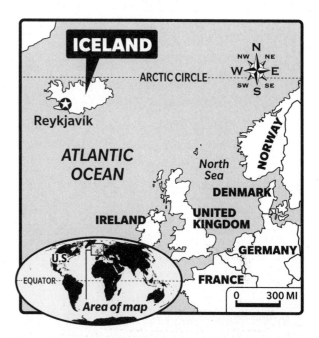

A geothermal plant next to a hot spring

6   Today, rivers of magma still boil beneath Iceland's surface. A major volcanic eruption happens there about every three years.

7   Iceland's underground volcanic activity also creates pools of steam water called hot springs. The steam from these hot springs is used to create geothermal energy.

8   Geothermal power is a renewable resource. That means it can never be used up because the supply of heat from within Earth is endless. Using renewable energy is cleaner than burning coal or natural gas, which creates pollution.

Making a Connection

9   Many countries in Europe want to switch to geothermal power. The proposed undersea cable would first link Iceland to the United Kingdom. Then the cable would link Iceland to the rest of Europe, about 1,200 miles away.

10 The idea for an electrical cable connecting Iceland to Europe has been discussed for years. But officials in Europe had thought it would be too expensive. Now, nations in Europe are willing to pay more for renewable energy to protect the environment.

Name: _____

Directions: Read the article "For Sale: Volcanic Power." Then answer the questions below.

1. Which detail is most important to include in a summary of the article?

A. Iceland's government wants to sell the unused energy to its neighbors across the Atlantic. *(paragraph 3)*

B. When you hear the name *Iceland*, you may think of ice and snow. *(paragraph 2)*

C. The islands of Hawaii formed in a similar way. *(paragraph 5)*

D. A major volcanic eruption happens there about every three years. *(paragraph 6)*

2. How does the map add to the reader's understanding of the article's main idea?

A. It shows that Iceland is an island with active volcanoes.

B. It shows where the capital of Iceland is located.

C. It shows the size of Iceland compared with that of other European countries.

D. It shows the distance between Iceland and the rest of Europe.

3. Which detail from the passage best supports the answer to question 2?

A. But this island nation is made up of more than 30 active volcanoes. *(paragraph 2)*

B. Iceland formed when molten rock gushed from the ocean floor and cooled . . . *(paragraph 5)*

C. Then the cable would link Iceland to the rest of Europe, about 1,200 miles away. *(paragraph 9)*

D. Now, nations in Europe are willing to pay more for renewable energy to protect the environment. *(paragraph 10)*

4. On the chart, describe one cause and one effect of geothermal energy produced in Iceland.

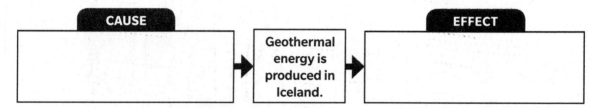

CAUSE	Geothermal energy is produced in Iceland.	EFFECT

5. How does the author support the idea that Iceland produces more energy than it uses?

A. By stating the population of Iceland

B. By explaining what a renewable resource is

C. By describing how Iceland formed

D. By comparing sources of energy used in the U.S. with those used in Iceland

6. Based on the article, which conclusion can be drawn about Iceland?

A. It consumes more energy than most countries.

B. Its government prefers not to deal with other countries.

C. It produces a lot of pollution through its geothermal power plants.

D. It has enough energy to sell to mainland Europe for many years to come.

China's Ancient Army

1   In 1974, farmers in China were digging a well. Suddenly they uncovered a life-sized statue of a soldier. It turned out, there were more. Since then, archaeologists have dug up a whole army in the area. They are all made of terra-cotta, or baked clay.

2   The statues came from the tomb of China's first emperor. Experts are amazed at how real they look. Each clay warrior is dressed differently. Each has a **unique** face and hairstyle. Some experts think the statues may look exactly like the soldiers who protected the powerful ruler.

Forever on Guard

3   Emperor Qin Shi Huangdi (chin shuh hwong-dee) ruled more than 2,200 years ago. He defeated six rival kingdoms. As a result, he united China for the first time.

4   When Qin died, he was buried in an underground palace. Experts believe the terra-cotta warriors were supposed to guard the emperor.

5   Many experts have wondered: Did sculptors model the statues after actual

One of the pits containing the statues is nearly the size of three football fields.

soldiers in Qin's army? To find out, a team of scientists took photos of some of the statues' ears. Why ears? In real life, no two human ears are the same.

6   "They act a bit like individual fingerprints," explains Andrew Bevan, an archaeologist.

7   The scientists have compared the ears of 30 statues. Each one is different. So it's possible the statues were made to look like real soldiers.

Hidden Tomb

8   Archaeologists believe there may be about 8,000 statues in all. So far, they have found only about 2,000. Most of the tomb is still deep underground. So is the body of the emperor. But if archaeologists get to dig that area one day, they'll have to be careful. Legend says Qin's tomb is booby-trapped to keep people away.

RUSSIA

KAZAKHSTAN

MONGOLIA

Beijing ✪

CHINA

Site of terra-cotta warriors

Xi'an ●

NORTH KOREA

SOUTH KOREA

JAPAN

Shanghai ●

East China Sea

INDIA

Hong Kong ●

TAIWAN

MYANMAR (BURMA)

LAOS

South China Sea

VIETNAM

N W E S

U.S.

EQUATOR

Area of map

Key

✪ National capital

● City

Name: _____

Directions: Read the article "China's Ancient Army." Then answer the questions below.

1. **Which sentence describes something Emperor Qin accomplished during his reign?**
   A. He defeated six rival kingdoms and united China for the first time.
   B. He discovered a life-sized statue of a soldier.
   c. He was buried in an underground palace.
   D. He uncovered the secrets of a terra-cotta army.

2. **Why do experts think Qin had terra-cotta soldiers placed in his underground palace?**
   A. To show what life was like in ancient China
   B. To make the palace more beautiful
   c. To guard the tomb and protect him in the afterlife
   D. To preserve images of his soldiers

3. **What is the opposite of the word *unique* in paragraph 2?**
   A. Common
   B. Special
   c. One-of-a-kind
   D. Strange

4. **Why did archaeologists take photos of the statues' ears?**
   A. The ears are the oldest parts of the sculptures.
   B. They wanted to analyze the materials used to make the statues.
   c. The ears are the easiest part of the statues to photograph.
   D. They were testing their theory about whether the statues were modeled after actual soldiers.

5. **Which of the following details best supports the reason the archaeologists chose to study the ears over other body parts?**
   A. Each clay warrior is dressed differently. Each has a unique face and hairstyle. *(paragraph 2)*
   B. "They act a bit like individual fingerprints." *(paragraph 6)*
   c. Experts are amazed at how real they look. *(paragraph 2)*
   D. Suddenly they uncovered a life-sized statue of a soldier. *(paragraph 1)*

6. **In the section "Hidden Tomb," what additional details does the author provide about Qin's tomb? Based on these details, what can you infer about Qin? Use evidence from the text to support your answer.**

   _____

   _____

   _____

   _____

China's Ancient Army

1   In 1974, farmers digging a well in China made a surprising discovery. They found a life-sized statue of a soldier. It turned out to be one of thousands. Since then, archaeologists have uncovered a whole army of soldiers in the area. They are all made of terra-cotta, or baked clay.

2   The statues came from the tomb of China's first emperor. Experts are amazed at how realistic they look. Each clay warrior is dressed differently and has a unique face and hairstyle. Some experts believe the statues look exactly like the soldiers who protected the powerful ruler.

Forever on Guard

3   Emperor Qin Shi Huangdi (chin shuh hwong-dee) ruled more than 2,200 years ago. He united China for the first time by defeating six rival kingdoms.

4   During his reign, Qin had about 700,000 workers build an underground palace. He planned to be buried there after he died. Experts believe the terra-cotta warriors were supposed to guard the tomb and protect Qin.

One of the pits containing the statues is nearly the size of three football fields.

The emperor thought he'd continue to rule in the afterlife.

5   Many experts have wondered: Did sculptors model the statues after actual soldiers in Qin's army? To test that theory, a team of scientists took digital photos of some of the statues' ears. Why ears? In real life, no two human ears are the same.

6   "They act a bit like individual fingerprints," explains archaeologist Andrew Bevan.

7   The scientists have compared the ears of 30 statues. They've found that each one is different. That means it's possible the statues were modeled after real-life soldiers.

Hidden Tomb

8   Archaeologists believe there are about 8,000 statues in all. So far, they have found only about 2,000. Most of the tomb is still deep underground. So is the body of the emperor. But if archaeologists get to **excavate** that area one day, they'll have to be careful. Legend says Qin's tomb is booby-trapped to keep people away.

Key
- ★ National capital
- • City

Name: _____

Directions: Read the article "China's Ancient Army." Then answer the questions below.

1. **Which sentence describes something Emperor Qin Shi Huangdi accomplished during his reign?**
    A. He uncovered the secrets of a terra-cotta army.
    B. He discovered a life-sized statue of a soldier.
    c. He united China for the first time by conquering six rival kingdoms.
    D. He was buried in an underground palace.

2. **Why do experts think Qin had terra-cotta soldiers placed in his underground palace?**
    A. To preserve images of his soldiers
    B. To guard the tomb and protect him in the afterlife
    c. To show what life was like in ancient China
    D. To make the palace more beautiful

3. **What is the meaning of** *excavate* **in paragraph 8?**
    A. Guard carefully   c. Protect from danger
    B. Conquer with violence   D. Uncover by digging

4. **Why did archaeologists take photos of the statues' ears?**
    A. The ears are the easiest part of the statues to photograph.
    B. They were testing their theory about whether the statues were modeled after actual soldiers.
    c. The ears are the oldest parts of the sculptures.
    D. They wanted to analyze the materials used to make the statues.

5. **Which of the following details best supports the reason the archaeologists chose to study the ears over other body parts?**
    A. "They act a bit like individual fingerprints." *(paragraph 6)*
    B. Each clay warrior is dressed differently and has a unique face and hairstyle. *(paragraph 2)*
    c. Experts are amazed at how realistic they look. *(paragraph 2)*
    D. [Farmers] found a life-sized statue of a soldier. *(paragraph 1)*

6. **In the section "Hidden Tomb," what additional details does the author provide about Qin's tomb? Based on these details, what can you infer about Qin? Use evidence from the text to support your answer.**

    _____

    _____

    _____

    _____

China's Ancient Army

1   In 1974, farmers digging a well in China made a surprising discovery: a life-sized statue of a soldier. It turned out to be one of thousands. Over the years, archaeologists have uncovered a whole army made of terra-cotta, or baked clay, in the area.

2   The statues are from the tomb of China's first emperor. Experts are amazed at how realistic they look. Each clay warrior is dressed differently and has a unique face and hairstyle. Some experts believe the statues may have been made to look exactly like the soldiers who protected China's powerful ruler.

Forever on Guard

3   Emperor Qin Shi Huangdi (chin shuh hwong-dee) came to power more than 2,200 years ago. In 221 B.C., he united China for the first time by conquering six rival kingdoms.

4   During his reign, Qin had about 700,000 workers build an elaborate underground palace. He would be buried here after he died. Experts believe the army of terra-cotta warriors was meant to guard the tomb and protect Qin. The emperor thought he'd continue to rule in the afterlife.

One of the pits containing the statues is nearly the size of three football fields.

5   Many experts have wondered if sculptors used actual soldiers in Qin's army as models for the lifelike statues. To test that theory, a team of scientists from China and Great Britain took digital photos of some of the statues' ears. Why ears? One reason is that in real life, no two human ears are the same.

6   "They act a bit like individual fingerprints," explains archaeologist Andrew Bevan.

7   The scientists have compared the ears of 30 statues. They've found that each one is unique. That means it's possible the statues were modeled after real-life soldiers.

Hidden Tomb

8   Archaeologists could be uncovering secrets of the terra-cotta army for years to come. They believe there are about 8,000 statues in all. So far, they have uncovered only about 2,000. Most of the tomb is still deep underground. So is the body of the emperor. But if archaeologists get to **excavate** that area one day, they'll have to be careful. Legend has it that Qin's tomb is booby-trapped with arrows to keep people from entering.

RUSSIA

KAZAKHSTAN

MONGOLIA

Beijing

CHINA

NORTH KOREA

Site of terra-cotta warriors

Xi'an

SOUTH KOREA

JAPAN

Shanghai

East China Sea

INDIA

Hong Kong

TAIWAN

MYANMAR (BURMA)

LAOS

South China Sea

VIETNAM

U.S.

EQUATOR

Area of map

Key

★ National capital
• City

Name: _____

Directions: Read the article "China's Ancient Army." Then answer the questions below.

1. **Which sentence describes something Emperor Qin Shi Huangdi accomplished during his reign?**

   A. He discovered a life-sized statue of a soldier.

   B. He united China for the first time by conquering six rival kingdoms.

   C. He uncovered the secrets of a terra-cotta army.

   D. He was buried in an underground palace.

2. **Why do experts think Qin had terra-cotta soldiers placed in his underground palace?**

   A. To guard the tomb and protect him in the afterlife

   B. To show what life was like in ancient China

   C. To make the palace more beautiful

   D. To preserve images of his soldiers

3. **What is the meaning of *excavate* in paragraph 8?**

   A. Guard carefully   C. Uncover by digging

   B. Protect from danger   D. Conquer with violence

4. **Why did archaeologists take photos of the statues' ears?**

   A. They wanted to analyze the materials used to make the statues.

   B. The ears are the oldest parts of the sculptures.

   C. They were testing their theory about whether the statues were modeled after actual soldiers.

   D. The ears are the easiest part of the statues to photograph.

5. **Which of the following details best supports the reason the archaeologists chose to study the ears over other body parts?**

   A. Each clay warrior is dressed differently and has a unique face and hairstyle. *(paragraph 2)*

   B. Experts are amazed at how realistic they look. *(paragraph 2)*

   C. In 1974, farmers . . . made a surprising discovery: a life-sized statue of a soldier. *(paragraph 1)*

   D. "They act a bit like individual fingerprints." *(paragraph 6)*

6. **In the section "Hidden Tomb," what additional details does the author provide about Qin's tomb? Based on these details, what can you infer about Qin? Use evidence from the text to support your answer.**

   _____

   _____

   _____

   _____

A Modern-Day Gold Rush

1   In 1849, thousands of people flocked to California. Why? They hoped to discover gold. In 2011, 12-year-old Gatlin Grove followed that same dream.

2   Gatlin headed out to Stanislaus River with his parents and two siblings. They were there to dig for gold—and to experience a bit of history.

3   People who searched for gold during the original California Gold Rush were called prospectors. Just like them, Gatlin and his family panned in streams. They used a box with a screen to sift gold out of dirt and water.

4   "It was really fun," Gatlin said. "You have to work pretty hard. But it pays off." He sold the shiny specks he collected—about $35 worth—to help buy a video game.

Cash for Gold

5   Gatlin was looking for gold mainly for the thrill. For many people, however, gold has become serious business.

6   The price of gold hit a record high in 2011. A person could get about $1,900 for an ounce of gold. That's about the size of an acorn.

7   Those record prices stirred a gold frenzy. People are always looking for new ways to make money. They began searching their jewelry boxes for gold to sell for cash.

8   Rising gold prices also inspired a new generation of dreamers to head west. They thought they might strike it rich there. These modern-day prospectors remind many people of the original miners in California. Some old gold mines there reopened in recent years.

9   "There is a history to it," explains Brad Jones of the Gold Prospectors Association of America. "California was really built on the Gold Rush."

The Forty-Niners

10   In 1848, a carpenter was building a sawmill in California for a man named John Sutter. The carpenter found a gold nugget near the American River. News of the discovery at Sutter's Mill spread worldwide. By 1849, people were pouring into California in search of gold. They became known as "the **forty-niners**," after the year the Gold Rush began. (That's where the San Francisco 49ers football team got its name.)

11   Some prospectors got rich. But most didn't. Mining was hard work. Many people spent much of their money on tools and other necessities. Some of the most successful people weren't miners. They were those who sold supplies to the miners. Others opened inns, banks, and other businesses. This helped California grow.

12   New towns sprang up and grew quickly. In 1848, about 6,000 people lived in San Francisco. In 1850, its population jumped to 25,000. That same year, California became the 31st state.

13   Not surprisingly, California is nicknamed the Golden State. It's motto—*Eureka!*—comes from a Greek word meaning "I have found it!" It captures the thrill of those early gold seekers. Today's prospectors share that same excitement.

The California Gold Rush

PACIFIC OCEAN
Sacramento River
Sutter's Mill
Lake Tahoe
NV
Sacramento ★
American River
CA
North Fork
Middle Fork
Stanislaus River ➤
South Fork
San Francisco

★ State capital
Scale: 0   25 MI

OR
ID
MT
WY
CA
NV
UT
CO
AZ
NM
Area of map

Name: _____

Directions: Read the article "A Modern-Day Gold Rush."
Then answer the questions below.

1. In paragraph 7, what does the phrase "stirred a gold frenzy" mean?

    A. Made it difficult to search for gold   **c.** Slowed the sale of gold

    B. Caused people to be excited about gold   **D.** Reminded people of the past

2. Which sentence from the article best supports the answer to question 1?

    A. These modern-day prospectors remind many people of the original miners in California. *(paragraph 8)*

    B. They used a box with a screen to sift gold out of dirt and water. *(paragraph 3)*

    c. The price of gold hit a record high in 2011. *(paragraph 6)*

    D. They began searching their jewelry boxes for gold to sell for cash. *(paragraph 7)*

3. The author uses a quotation from Brad Jones. He states, "California was really built on the Gold Rush." How does the author support this claim?

    A. By comparing a historical event with a modern-day event

    B. By providing an anecdote that uses strong emotional language

    c. By describing important events in the order in which they happened

    D. By explaining a problem and describing a possible solution

4. According to the article, why were gold prospectors called "the forty-niners"?

    A. They were named after the year the Gold Rush began.

    B. They were named after the San Francisco football team.

    c. Gold at the time sold for $49 an ounce.

    D. California was the 49th state.

5. Complete the chart by describing one cause and one effect of the original California Gold Rush.

CAUSE   People poured into California in search of gold.   EFFECT

6. What is the main purpose of the article?

    A. To describe a recent trend that reminds people of a historical event

    B. To explain how California became a state

    c. To describe the difficulties of panning for gold

    D. To explain why gold prices went up in 2011

A Modern-Day Gold Rush

1   In 1849, thousands of people flocked to California. Why? They hoped to discover gold. In 2011, 12-year-old Gatlin Grove followed that same dream.

2   Gatlin headed out to Stanislaus River with his parents and two siblings. They were there to dig for gold—and to experience a bit of history.

3   People who searched for gold during the original California Gold Rush were called prospectors. Just like them, Gatlin and his family panned in streams. They used a box with a screen to sift gold out of dirt and water.

4   "It was really fun," Gatlin said. "You have to work pretty hard, but it pays off." He sold the shiny specks he collected—about $35 worth—to help buy a video game.

Cash for Gold

5   Gatlin was panning for gold mainly for the thrill. For many people, however, gold has become serious business.

6   The price of gold hit a record high in 2011. An ounce of gold (about the size of an acorn) was worth about $1,900.

7   Those record prices stirred a gold frenzy. During tough economic times, people look for new ways to make money. People across the country began scouring their jewelry boxes for gold to sell for cash.

8   Rising gold prices also inspired a new generation of dreamers to head west with thoughts of striking it rich. These modern-day prospectors remind many people of the original miners in California. Some old gold mines there reopened in recent years.

9   "There is a history to it," explains Brad Jones of the Gold Prospectors Association of America. "California was really built on the Gold Rush."

The Forty-Niners

10   In 1848, a carpenter was building a sawmill in California for a man named John Sutter. The carpenter found a gold nugget near the American River. News of the discovery at Sutter's Mill spread worldwide. By 1849, people were pouring into California in search of gold. They became known as "the **forty-niners**," after the year the Gold Rush began. (That's where the San Francisco 49ers football team got its name.)

11   Some prospectors got rich, but most didn't. Mining was hard work. Many people spent much of their money on tools and other necessities. Some of the most successful people weren't miners but those who sold supplies to the miners. Others opened inns, banks, and other businesses that helped California grow.

12   New towns sprang up and grew quickly. San Francisco's population jumped from 6,000 people in 1848 to 25,000 in 1850. That same year, California became the 31st state.

13   Not surprisingly, California is nicknamed the Golden State. It's motto—*Eureka!*—comes from a Greek word meaning "I have found it!" It captures the thrill of those early gold seekers. Today's prospectors share that same excitement.

The California Gold Rush

Name: _____

Directions: Read the article "A Modern-Day Gold Rush."
Then answer the questions below.

1. In paragraph 7, what does the phrase "stirred a gold frenzy" mean?

   A. Slowed the sale of gold

   B. Made it difficult to search for gold

   c. Caused people to be excited about gold

   D. Reminded people of the past

2. Which sentence from the article best supports the answer to question 1?

   A. The price of gold hit a record high in 2011. *(paragraph 6)*

   B. These modern-day prospectors remind many people of the original miners in California. *(paragraph 8)*

   c. People across the country began scouring their jewelry boxes for gold to sell for cash. *(paragraph 7)*

   D. They used a box with a screen to sift gold out of dirt and water. *(paragraph 3)*

3. The author uses a quotation from Brad Jones. He states, "California was really built on the Gold Rush." How does the author support this claim?

   A. By comparing a historical event with a modern-day event

   B. By providing an anecdote that uses strong emotional language

   c. By explaining a problem and describing a possible solution

   D. By describing important events in the order in which they happened

4. According to the article, why were gold prospectors called "the forty-niners"?

   A. California was the 49th state.

   B. They were named after the year the Gold Rush began.

   c. Gold at the time sold for $49 an ounce.

   D. They were named after the San Francisco football team.

5. Complete the chart by describing one cause and one effect of the original California Gold Rush.

CAUSE		EFFECT
	People poured into California in search of gold.	

6. What is the main purpose of the article?

   A. To explain how California became a state

   B. To describe the difficulties of panning for gold

   c. To explain why gold prices went up in 2011

   D. To describe a recent trend that reminds people of a historical event

A Modern-Day Gold Rush

1   More than 160 years ago, thousands of people flocked to California with the hope of discovering gold. In 2011, 12-year-old Gatlin Grove from Frazier Park, California, followed that same dream.

2   Gatlin headed out to Stanislaus River, along with his parents and two siblings. They were there to dig for gold—and to experience a bit of history.

3   People who searched for gold during the original California Gold Rush were called prospectors. Just like them, Gatlin and his family panned in streams. They used a box with a screen to sift gold out of dirt and water.

4   "It was really fun," Gatlin said. "You have to work pretty hard, but it pays off." He sold the shiny specks he collected—about $35 worth—to help buy a video game.

Cash for Gold

5   Gatlin was panning for gold mainly for the thrill. For many people, however, gold has become serious business.

6   The price of gold hit a record high in 2011, when an ounce (about the size of an acorn) was worth about $1,900.

7   Those record prices stirred a gold frenzy. During tough economic times, people look for new ways to make money. People across the country began scouring their jewelry boxes for gold to sell for cash.

8   Rising gold prices also inspired a new generation of dreamers to head west with thoughts of striking it rich. These modern-day prospectors remind many people of the original miners in California. Some old gold mines there reopened in recent years.

9   "There is a history to it," explains Brad Jones of the Gold Prospectors Association of America. "California was really built on the Gold Rush."

The Forty-Niners

10   In 1848, a carpenter found a gold nugget while building a sawmill for a man named John Sutter near the American River in California. News of the discovery at Sutter's Mill spread worldwide. By 1849, people were pouring into California in search of gold. They became known as "the **forty-niners**," after the year the Gold Rush began. (That's where the San Francisco 49ers football team got its name.)

11   Some prospectors got rich, but most didn't. Mining was hard work, and many people spent much of their money on tools and other necessities. Some of the most successful people weren't miners but those who sold supplies to the miners. Others opened inns, banks, and other businesses that helped California grow.

12   New towns sprang up and grew quickly. San Francisco's population jumped from 6,000 people in 1848 to 25,000 in 1850. That same year, California became the 31st state.

13   Not surprisingly, California is nicknamed the Golden State. It's motto—*Eureka!*—comes from a Greek word meaning "I have found it!" It captures the thrill of those early gold seekers. Today's prospectors share that same excitement.

The California Gold Rush

★ State capital

Scale: 0   25 MI

Area of map

Name: _____

Directions: Read the article "A Modern-Day Gold Rush."
Then answer the questions below.

1. In paragraph 7, what does the phrase "stirred a gold frenzy" mean?

   A. Caused people to be excited about gold

   B. Made it difficult to search for gold

   c. Slowed the sale of gold

   D. Reminded people of the past

2. Which sentence from the article best supports the answer to question 1?

   A. These modern-day prospectors remind many people of the original miners in California. *(paragraph 8)*

   B. People across the country began scouring their jewelry boxes for gold to sell for cash. *(paragraph 7)*

   c. They used a box with a screen to sift gold out of dirt and water. *(paragraph 3)*

   D. The price of gold hit a record high in 2011 . . . *(paragraph 6)*

3. The author uses a quotation from Brad Jones. He states, "California was really built on the Gold Rush." How does the author support this claim?

   A. By describing important events in the order in which they happened

   B. By comparing a historical event with a modern-day event

   c. By providing an anecdote that uses strong emotional language

   D. By explaining a problem and describing a possible solution

4. According to the article, why were gold prospectors called "the forty-niners"?

   A. They were named after the San Francisco football team.

   B. California was the 49th state.

   c. Gold at the time sold for $49 an ounce.

   D. They were named after the year the Gold Rush began.

5. Complete the chart by describing one cause and one effect of the original California Gold Rush.

CAUSE		EFFECT
	People poured into California in search of gold.	

6. What is the main purpose of the article?

   A. To explain how California became a state

   B. To describe a recent trend that reminds people of a historical event

   c. To describe the difficulties of panning for gold

   D. To explain why gold prices went up in 2011

Powerful Words

1   *Four score and seven years ago . . .* You've probably heard this famous phrase before. It's the beginning of the Gettysburg Address. President Abraham Lincoln delivered this powerful speech on November 19, 1863. He was honoring Union soldiers who had died in the Battle of Gettysburg. This battle was fought during the U.S. Civil War. Lincoln spoke for less than three minutes. But we still remember his words more than 150 years later.

A Divided Nation

2   The Civil War was fought between the Northern states (the Union) and the Southern states (the Confederacy). The two sides couldn't agree on many issues. But the most important issue was slavery. Eleven Southern states didn't want to give up owning slaves. So they **seceded** from the United States. They left and formed a new nation. President Lincoln led the Union. He wanted to keep all the states together as one nation.

3   The North and the South fought many battles. The bloodiest battle was at Gettysburg, Pennsylvania. Soldiers there fought for three days in July 1863. Finally, the Union forces defeated the Confederate Army. More than 50,000 soldiers were killed or wounded.

4   The Battle of Gettysburg was a turning point in the war. The Confederate Army was forced back into the South.

A Special Speech

5   In November 1863, Lincoln traveled to Gettysburg. He spoke at the opening of a cemetery for Union soldiers. Lincoln explained why winning the war was so important for the Union. He said the Founding Fathers had created a nation where people were free to choose their leaders. This nation must not be torn apart. Lincoln said "that government of the people, by the people, for the people, shall not perish from the earth."

6   In April 1865, the Confederacy surrendered. Sadly, Lincoln was killed just days after the war ended. But the message of his famous speech lives on.

7   "We find meaning in it today because it [expresses] values that people still hold dear," says Caroline Janney, an expert on the Civil War.

Abraham Lincoln delivering his speech at Gettysburg

Name: _____

Directions: Read the article "Powerful Words." Then answer the questions below.

1. According to "Powerful Words," what was the main purpose of Lincoln's Gettysburg Address?

    A. To convince the Confederacy to surrender

    B. To honor Union soldiers and explain what they were fighting for

    C. To declare a Union victory in the Civil War

    D. To officially outlaw slavery

2. Which is the most likely reason the author includes a quote by Caroline Janney?

    A. To show that Abraham Lincoln was determined to keep the United States together

    B. To explain what the Union Army was fighting for

    C. To explain why the Gettysburg Address is still powerful today

    D. To support the idea that the Gettysburg Address was not understood at the time it was delivered

3. Which of the following states a cause of the Civil War?

    A. The two sides couldn't agree on many issues. But the most important issue was slavery. *(paragraph 2)*

    B. More than 50,000 soldiers were killed or wounded. *(paragraph 3)*

    C. [President Abraham Lincoln] was honoring Union soldiers who had died in the Battle of Gettysburg. *(paragraph 1)*

    D. Finally, the Union forces defeated the Confederate Army. *(paragraph 3)*

4. What is the purpose of the section "A Divided Nation"?

    A. To summarize what Lincoln said in the Gettysburg Address

    B. To compare the Gettysburg Address to other key events in the Civil War

    C. To give information about the Civil War and the battle that took place in Gettysburg

    D. To describe the effects of the Gettysburg Address on the Union and the Confederacy

5. As it is used in paragraph 2, the phrase "seceded from" means _____.

    A. joined with   **C.** defeated

    B. surrendered to   **D.** split from

6. The Battle of Gettysburg and the Gettysburg Address were key events during the Civil War. On a separate sheet of paper, explain why each event was important. Use details from the article to support your answer.

Powerful Words

1   *Four score and seven years ago . . .* You've probably heard this famous phrase before. It's the first line of the Gettysburg Address, one of the greatest speeches in American history. President Abraham Lincoln delivered this speech on November 19, 1863. He was honoring Union soldiers who had died in the Battle of Gettysburg during the U.S. Civil War. Lincoln spoke for less than three minutes. But we still remember his powerful words more than 150 years later.

A Divided Nation

2   The Civil War was fought between the Northern states (the Union) and the Southern states (the Confederacy). The two sides disagreed over many issues, especially slavery. Eleven Southern states didn't want to give up owning slaves. They **seceded** from the United States and formed a new nation. President Lincoln led the Union. He wanted to keep all the states together as one nation.

3   The North and the South fought many battles. The bloodiest was fought at Gettysburg, Pennsylvania, in July 1863. Soldiers fought for three days. Finally, the Union forces defeated the Confederate Army, led by General Robert E. Lee.

4   The battle was a turning point in the war. Lee's army was forced back into the South. But victory came at a huge cost for both sides. More than 50,000 soldiers were killed or wounded.

A Special Speech

5   In November 1863, Lincoln traveled to Gettysburg. He spoke at the opening of a cemetery for Union soldiers. Lincoln explained why winning the war was so important for the Union. He talked about how the Founding Fathers had created a nation where people were free to choose their leaders. He stressed that the nation must not be torn apart. Lincoln said that the "government of the people, by the people, for the people shall not perish from the earth."

6   In April 1865, the Confederacy surrendered. Sadly, Lincoln was killed just days after the war ended. But the message of his famous speech lives on.

7   "We find meaning in it today because it [expresses] values that people still hold dear," says Civil War expert Caroline Janney.

Abraham Lincoln delivering his speech at Gettysburg

Name: _____

Directions: Read the article "Powerful Words." Then answer the questions below.

1. According to "Powerful Words," what was the main purpose of Lincoln's Gettysburg Address?

    A. To convince the Confederacy to surrender

    B. To declare a Union victory in the Civil War

    C. To honor Union soldiers and explain what they were fighting for

    D. To officially outlaw slavery

2. Which is the most likely reason the author includes a quote by Caroline Janney?

    A. To explain why the Gettysburg Address is still powerful today

    B. To clarify what the Union Army was fighting for

    C. To show that Abraham Lincoln was determined to keep the United States together

    D. To support the idea that the Gettysburg Address was not understood at the time it was delivered

3. Which of the following states a cause of the Civil War?

    A. [President Abraham Lincoln] was honoring Union soldiers who had died in the Battle of Gettysburg during the U.S. Civil War. *(paragraph 1)*

    B. Finally, the Union forces defeated the Confederate Army, led by General Robert E. Lee. *(paragraph 3)*

    C. More than 50,000 soldiers were killed or wounded. *(paragraph 4)*

    D. The two sides disagreed over many issues, especially slavery. *(paragraph 2)*

4. What is the purpose of the section "A Divided Nation"?

    A. To describe the effects of the Gettysburg Address on the Union and the Confederacy

    B. To compare the Gettysburg Address to other key events in the Civil War

    C. To summarize what Lincoln said in the Gettysburg Address

    D. To give information about the Civil War and the battle that took place in Gettysburg

5. As it is used in paragraph 2, the phrase "seceded from" means _____.

    A. surrendered to   **C.** split from

    B. joined with   **D.** defeated

6. The Battle of Gettysburg and the Gettysburg Address were key events during the Civil War. On a separate sheet of paper, explain why each event was important. Use details from the article to support your answer.

Powerful Words

1   *Four score and seven years ago . . .* You've probably heard this famous phrase before. It's the first line of the Gettysburg Address, one of the greatest speeches in American history. President Abraham Lincoln delivered this speech on November 19, 1863, to honor Union soldiers who had died in the Battle of Gettysburg during the U.S. Civil War. Lincoln spoke for less than three minutes. But we still remember his powerful words more than 150 years later.

A Divided Nation

2   The Civil War was fought between the Northern states (the Union) and the Southern states (the Confederacy). The two sides disagreed over many issues, especially slavery. Eleven Southern states didn't want to give up owning slaves. They **seceded** from the United States to form a new nation. President Lincoln, who led the Union, wanted to keep all the states together as one nation.

3   The North and the South fought many battles. The bloodiest was fought at Gettysburg, Pennsylvania, in July 1863. After three days of fighting, Union forces defeated the Confederate Army, led by General Robert E. Lee.

4   The battle was a turning point in the war. The Union victory forced Lee's army back into the South. But victory came at a huge cost for both sides. More than 50,000 soldiers were killed or wounded.

A Special Speech

5   In November 1863, Lincoln went to Gettysburg to speak at the opening of a cemetery for Union soldiers. Lincoln talked about why winning the war was so important for the Union. He spoke about how the Founding Fathers had created a nation where people were free to choose their leaders— and how that nation must not be torn apart. He said that the "government of the people, by the people, for the people shall not perish from the earth."

6   In April 1865, the Confederacy surrendered. Sadly, Lincoln was killed just days after the war ended. But the message of his famous speech lives on.

7   "We find meaning in it today because it [expresses] values that people still hold dear," says Civil War expert Caroline Janney.

Abraham Lincoln delivering his speech at Gettysburg

Name: _____

Directions: Read the article "Powerful Words." Then answer the questions below.

1. According to "Powerful Words," what was the main purpose of Lincoln's Gettysburg Address?

   A. To convince the Confederacy to surrender

   B. To declare a Union victory in the Civil War

   C. To officially outlaw slavery

   D. To honor Union soldiers and explain what they were fighting for

2. Which is the most likely reason the author includes a quote by Caroline Janney?

   A. To clarify what the Union Army was fighting for

   B. To show that Abraham Lincoln was determined to keep the United States together

   C. To support the idea that the Gettysburg Address was not understood at the time it was delivered

   D. To explain why the Gettysburg Address is still powerful today

3. Which of the following states a cause of the Civil War?

   A. President Abraham Lincoln delivered this speech . . . to honor Union soldiers who had died in the Battle of Gettysburg during the U.S. Civil War. (*paragraph 1*)

   B. The two sides disagreed over many issues, especially slavery. (*paragraph 2*)

   C. After three days of fighting, Union forces defeated the Confederate Army, led by General Robert E. Lee. (*paragraph 3*)

   D. More than 50,000 soldiers were killed or wounded. (*paragraph 4*)

4. What is the purpose of the section "A Divided Nation"?

   A. To compare the Gettysburg Address to other key events in the Civil War

   B. To give information about the Civil War and the battle that took place in Gettysburg

   C. To describe the effects of the Gettysburg Address on the Union and the Confederacy

   D. To summarize what Lincoln said in the Gettysburg Address

5. As it is used in paragraph 2, the phrase "seceded from" means _____.

   A. split from   C. surrendered to

   B. joined with   D. defeated

6. The Battle of Gettysburg and the Gettysburg Address were key events during the Civil War. On a separate sheet of paper, explain why each event was important. Use details from the article to support your answer.

Searching for Amelia

Aviation pioneer Amelia Earhart

1   It was 1937. Amelia Earhart was already known around the world. She had set many high-flying records. She had become the first woman to fly solo across the Atlantic Ocean. On May 20 of that year, Earhart set out on an even more daring flight. She wanted to fly around the globe. But her plane vanished over the Pacific Ocean. What happened to Earhart and her navigator, Fred Noonan? For a long time, that remained a mystery. Now, researchers are finding new evidence that could help crack the case.

Island of Mystery

2   The search for Earhart is centered on Nikumaroro. This small island in the South Pacific is **uninhabited**. No people have lived there. But researchers have found artifacts, including pieces of a knife, that they think belonged to Earhart. Earhart and Noonan may have crash-landed near the island. They probably spent their final days as castaways there.

3   One possible clue is a photo of a shipwreck near the island. It was taken in October 1937. Historians noticed something sticking out of the water in the photo. They think it could be part of Earhart's plane.

High-Tech Hunt

4   Experts searched the area where the photo was taken. They used underwater robots to hunt for remains of Earhart and her plane.

5   The robots took images of the ocean floor. Months later, experts noticed one of these images showed a mysterious object. It looked like an airplane wing. It's the right size and shape to be part of Earhart's plane.

6   Now another group of experts plan to use submarines to search the area again. They want to find that mysterious object. They want to launch an expedition that would take them far below the surface of the sea. Will they finally solve the mystery?

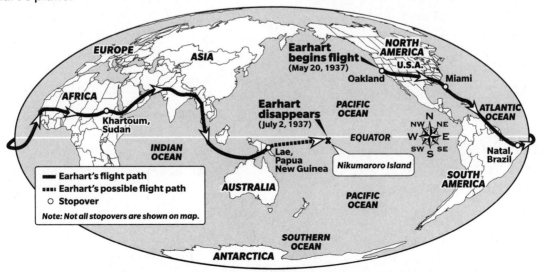

Name: _____

Directions: Read the article "Searching for Amelia." Then answer the questions below.

1. Label the events in the story from 1 to 4 in the order in which they took place.

___ Earhart's plane disappeared over the Pacific Ocean.

___ Researchers used robots to hunt for remains of Earhart's plane.

___ Photos were taken of a shipwreck near Nikumaroro.

___ Amelia Earhart flew solo across the Atlantic Ocean.

2. Explain two pieces of evidence that suggest that Earhart and Noonan crash-landed near Nikumaroro Island.

_____

_____

3. Read these sentences from the text and answer the question below.

> The search for Earhart is centered on Nikumaroro.
> This small island in the South Pacific is **uninhabited**.

What does the word *uninhabited* mean in the context of this passage?

A. Private

B. Lacking vegetation

C. Not lived on or in

D. Heavily populated

4. What text in the article gives you a context clue for the definition of *uninhabited*?

A. But researchers have found artifacts, including pieces of a knife . . . *(paragraph 2)*

B. Earhart and Noonan may have crash-landed near the island. *(paragraph 2)*

C. Historians noticed something sticking out of the water in the photo. *(paragraph 3)*

D. No people have lived there. *(paragraph 2)*

5. What proof has been found connecting Earhart to Nikumaroro?

A. No solid proof has been found yet.

B. A fork with her initials was found there.

C. Her plane's wing was seen in a photograph.

D. A wing of her plane was found there.

6. What does the dotted line on the map indicate?

A. The places that underwater vehicles are exploring

B. The part of Earhart's journey that experts are not certain about

C. Spots where Earhart's plane has been sighted

D. The flight path that Earhart is known to have taken

Searching for Amelia

1   It was 1937. Amelia Earhart was already famous all around the world. She had become the first woman to fly solo across the Atlantic Ocean. On May 20 of that year, she set out on an even more daring flight. She wanted to circle the globe. But over the Pacific Ocean, her plane vanished. What happened to Earhart and her navigator, Fred Noonan? For a long time, that remained a mystery. Now, researchers are finding new evidence that could help crack the case.

Aviation pioneer
Amelia Earhart

Island of Mystery

2   For the past two decades, the search for Earhart has centered on Nikumaroro. This small island in the South Pacific is **uninhabited**. No humans are known to have lived there. But researchers have found artifacts, including pieces of a knife, that they think belonged to Earhart. Earhart and Noonan may have crash-landed near the island. They probably spent their final days as castaways there.

3   One possible clue is a photo of a shipwreck near Nikumaroro. It was taken in October 1937. Historians noticed something sticking out of the water in the photo. They think it could be part of Earhart's plane.

High-Tech Hunt

4   Experts at recovering wrecks have searched the area where the photo was taken. They used high-tech underwater robots to hunt for remains of Earhart and her plane.

5   The robots took images of the ocean floor. In 2010, experts noticed that one of these images showed an object resembling a 22-foot-long airplane wing. When the image was first recorded, no one had seen the object. Months later someone finally noticed the mysterious clue in the photo. It's the right size and shape to be part of Earhart's plane.

6   Now experts at The International Group for Historic Aircraft Recovery plan to use submarines to search the area in the photograph again. They want to find that mysterious object. They are trying to raise enough money to launch a 30-day expedition that would take them 3,280 feet below the surface of the sea.

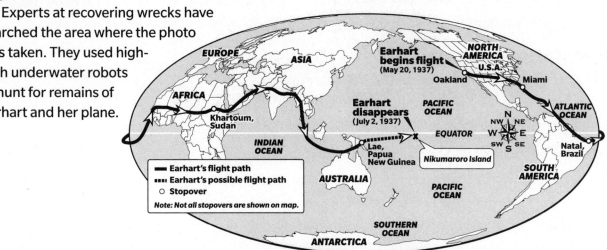

Name: _____

Directions: Read the article "Searching for Amelia." Then answer the questions below.

1. Label the events in the story from 1 to 4 in the order in which they took place.

____ Amelia Earhart flew solo across the Atlantic Ocean.

____ Photos were taken of a shipwreck near Nikumaroro.

____ Researchers used robots to hunt for remains of Earhart's plane.

____ Earhart's plane disappeared over the Pacific Ocean.

2. Explain two pieces of evidence that suggest that Earhart and Noonan crash-landed near Nikumaroro Island.

_____

_____

3. Read these sentences from the text and answer the question below.

> For the past two decades, the search for Earhart has centered on Nikumaroro. This small island in the South Pacific is **uninhabited**.

What does the word *uninhabited* mean in the context of this passage?

A. Lacking vegetation

B. Heavily populated

c. Not lived on or in

D. Private

4. What text in the article gives you a context clue for the definition of *uninhabited*?

A. No humans are known to have lived there. *(paragraph 2)*

B. But researchers have found artifacts, including pieces of a knife . . . *(paragraph 2)*

c. Earhart and Noonan may have crash-landed near the island. *(paragraph 2)*

D. Historians noticed something sticking out of the water in the photo. *(paragraph 3)*

5. What proof has been found connecting Earhart to Nikumaroro?

A. A fork with her initials was found there.

B. A wing of her plane was found there.

c. Her plane's wing was seen in a photograph.

D. No solid proof has been found yet.

6. What is the purpose of the subheadings in the article?

_____

_____

7. What does the dotted line on the map indicate?

A. The part of Earhart's journey that experts are not certain about

B. The flight path that Earhart is known to have taken

c. The places that underwater vehicles are exploring

D. Spots where Earhart's plane has been sighted

Searching for Amelia

1   By 1937, Amelia Earhart's high-flying feats had made her world-famous. She had become the first woman to fly solo across the Atlantic Ocean. On May 20 of that year, she set out on an even more daring flight. She wanted to circle the globe. But over the Pacific Ocean, her plane vanished. What happened to Earhart and her navigator, Fred Noonan? For a long time, that remained a mystery. Now, a team of researchers is finding new evidence that could help crack the case.

Aviation pioneer
Amelia Earhart

Island of Mystery

2   For the past two decades, the search for Earhart has centered on Nikumaroro. This small island in the South Pacific is **uninhabited**. No humans are known to have lived there. But researchers have found artifacts, including pieces of a knife, that they think belonged to Earhart. They speculate that Earhart and Noonan crash-landed near the island. They probably spent their final days as castaways there.

3   One possible clue is a photo taken in October 1937 of a shipwreck near Nikumaroro. Historians noticed something sticking out of the water in the photo. They think it could be part of Earhart's plane.

experts noticed that one of these images showed an object resembling a 22-foot-long airplane wing. When the image was first recorded, no one had seen the object. Only months later did someone finally notice the mysterious clue in the photo. According to experts, it's the right size and shape to be part of Earhart's plane.

6   Now experts at The International Group for Historic Aircraft Recovery plan to use submarines to search the area in the photograph again for the mysterious object. They are trying to raise enough money to launch a 30-day expedition that would take them 3,280 feet below the surface of the sea.

High-Tech Hunt

4   Experts at recovering wrecks have searched the area where the photo was taken. They used high-tech underwater robots to hunt for remains of Earhart and her plane.

5   One task of these robots was taking images of the ocean floor. In 2010,

EUROPE   ASIA   Earhart begins flight (May 20, 1937)   NORTH AMERICA   U.S.A.   Oakland   Miami

AFRICA   Khartoum, Sudan   PACIFIC OCEAN   ATLANTIC OCEAN

Earhart disappears (July 2, 1937)   EQUATOR   INDIAN OCEAN   Lae, Papua New Guinea   Nikumaroro Island   Natal, Brazil

N NE NW W E SW SE S

— Earhart's flight path
▪▪▪▪ Earhart's possible flight path
○ Stopover
Note: Not all stopovers are shown on map.

AUSTRALIA   PACIFIC OCEAN   SOUTH AMERICA

SOUTHERN OCEAN

ANTARCTICA

Name: _____

Directions: Read the article "Searching for Amelia." Then answer the questions below.

1. Label the events in the story from 1 to 4 in the order in which they took place.

____ Photos were taken of a shipwreck near Nikumaroro.

____ Earhart's plane disappeared over the Pacific Ocean.

____ Researchers used robots to hunt for remains of Earhart's plane.

____ Amelia Earhart flew solo across the Atlantic Ocean.

2. Explain two pieces of evidence that suggest that Earhart and Noonan crash-landed near Nikumaroro Island.

_____

_____

3. Read these sentences from the text and answer the question below.

> For the past two decades, the search for Earhart has centered on Nikumaroro. This small island in the South Pacific is **uninhabited**.

What does the word *uninhabited* mean in the context of this passage?

A. Not lived on or in   c. Heavily populated

B. Lacking vegetation   D. Private

4. What text in the article gives you a context clue for the definition of *uninhabited*?

A. But researchers have found artifacts, including pieces of a knife . . . *(paragraph 2)*

B. They speculate that Earhart and Noonan crash-landed near the island. *(paragraph 2)*

c. No humans are known to have lived there. *(paragraph 2)*

D. Historians noticed something sticking out of the water in the photo. *(paragraph 3)*

5. What proof has been found connecting Earhart to Nikumaroro?

A. A fork with her initials was found there.   c. No solid proof has been found yet.

B. A wing of her plane was found there.   D. Her plane's wing was seen in a photograph.

6. What is the purpose of the subheadings in the article?

_____

_____

7. What does the dotted line on the map indicate?

A. The places that underwater vehicles are exploring

B. Spots where Earhart's plane has been sighted

c. The part of Earhart's journey that experts are not certain about

D. The flight path that Earhart is known to have taken

Death of a Boy-King

1   King Tutankhamen (TOO-tahn-KAH-mehn) was just 9 years old when he became the ruler of Egypt. The young pharaoh died only 10 years later. That was more than 3,300 years ago. But his story has fascinated the world since his tomb was discovered in 1922.

2   Scientists have since learned a lot about Tut. But one thing has remained a mystery: How did he die? Chris Naunton is the director of the Egypt Exploration Society. He believes he may have solved the puzzle. He studied nearly 100 years' worth of evidence to come up with his answer. He thinks the boy-king was killed in a chariot accident.

A Golden Discovery

3   Most people didn't know about Tut for a long time. Then archaeologist Howard Carter discovered Tut's tomb in Egypt. The tomb was filled with gold-covered furniture and other artifacts. In one room, Carter found a series of golden coffins. They were stacked one inside another. Inside the last coffin was King Tut's mummy. Long ago, Egyptians preserved people as mummies. They believed the dead would need their bodies in the afterlife.

4   Experts have wondered how Tut died. They had many theories, or ideas. Some thought he died from an infection from a broken leg and a blood disease. Naunton decided to try to crack the case himself.

Mummy Mystery

5   Naunton began by reading Carter's notes. Carter had written about his discovery of Tut in 1922. He noted that Tut's mummy wasn't prepared like most other mummies. For one thing, his chest had been stuffed with linen and other materials.

6   That made Naunton curious. So he studied old X-ray images of Tut's body. He saw that Tut's heart and some of his ribs were missing. What happened to them? Naunton thought maybe they were removed from Tut's body because they were badly damaged. But how?

Testing a Theory

7   Ancient Egyptian rulers often rode in horse-drawn chariots. Could Tut have died in a chariot crash? Naunton thought so. He decided to test that theory.

8   Naunton worked with some car-crash investigators. They created chariot accidents on computers. They found that getting hit by a chariot could crush a person's ribs and heart. Naunton believed he found his answer.

(continued)

One of King Tut's coffins

Case Closed?

9   Many archaeologists don't agree with Naunton. Some think Carter's team removed Tut's ribs. That would have made it easier for them to carry the mummy out of the tomb. Also, Tut wasn't the only pharaoh to be found without a heart. As for Tut's ribs, they might have been damaged by a kick from a horse.

10   Still, Naunton stands by his theory. "At this point, this is as good of a hypothesis that we have," he says. But, he adds, "I wouldn't want to think that this discussion is completely over."

HOW TO MAKE A MUMMY

The ancient Egyptians took about 70 days to prepare a body as a mummy. Only rulers and wealthy people got this treatment. Here's how it was done.

1. Remove the organs. The Egyptians usually left in the heart. Other organs were stored in special jars and buried with the mummy.

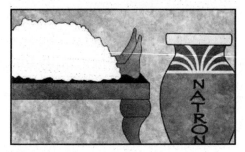

2. Add salt. Workers completely filled and covered the body with a type of salt, called natron. The natron dried out the body, helping to preserve it.

3. Wrap it up. After 40 days, workers washed the body and rubbed it with scented oils. Finally, they wrapped the body in strips of linen and placed it inside a special coffin, which was often decorated.

Name: _____

Directions: Read the article "Death of a Boy-King." Then answer the questions below.

1. What was the first step Chris Naunton took to try to figure out the cause of King Tut's death?

   A. He had scans taken of King Tut's mummy.

   B. He read the notes of the archaeologist who found Tut's tomb.

   C. He studied old X-rays of King Tut's skeleton.

   D. He had car-crash investigators create chariot crashes on computers.

2. Which detail from the article best supports the answer to question 1?

   A. Naunton began by reading Carter's notes. *(paragraph 5)*

   B. He saw that Tut's heart and some of his ribs were missing. *(paragraph 6)*

   C. Naunton thought maybe they were removed from Tut's body because they were badly damaged. *(paragraph 6)*

   D. Naunton worked with some car-crash investigators. *(paragraph 8)*

3. What does the phrase "crack the case" mean as it is used in paragraph 4?

   A. Work with car-crash investigators

   B. Break open King Tut's coffin

   C. Solve the mystery of King Tut's death

   D. Accept an assignment to study Tut's mummy

4. According to the article, how did King Tut's mummy differ from most other Egyptian mummies?

   A. His heart was missing, and his chest was stuffed with linen and other materials.

   B. It was placed in a special, decorated coffin.

   C. None of Tut's ribs were missing.

   D. His chest was stuffed with salt and still had his heart.

5. Which detail from the section "How to Make a Mummy" best supports the answer to question 4?

   A. Other organs were stored in special jars and buried with the mummy.

   B. Workers completely filled and covered the body with a type of salt, called natron.

   C. The Egyptians usually left in the heart.

   D. Finally, they . . . placed it inside a special coffin, which was often decorated.

6. What is the section "Case Closed?" mostly about?

   A. What scientists know about King Tut's life

   B. How mummies were made in ancient Egypt

   C. How King Tut's tomb was discovered

   D. Why some scientists don't think King Tut was killed in a chariot accident

Name: _____

7. In paragraph 10, Chris Naunton says, "I wouldn't want to think that this discussion is completely over." What do you think he means by that statement? Give details to support your answer.

_____

_____

_____

_____

_____

_____

_____

_____

_____

Death of a Boy-King

1   King Tutankhamen (TOO-tahn-KAH-mehn) was just 9 years old when he became the ruler of Egypt. The young pharaoh died only 10 years later. That was more than 3,300 years ago. But his story has fascinated the world since his tomb was discovered in 1922.

2   Scientists have since learned a lot about Tut. But one thing has remained a mystery: How did he die? Chris Naunton, director of the Egypt Exploration Society, believes he may have solved the puzzle. He studied nearly 100 years' worth of evidence to come up with his answer. He thinks the boy-king was killed in a chariot accident.

A Golden Discovery

3   Not much was known about Tut for a long time. Then British archaeologist Howard Carter discovered Tut's tomb in Egypt. It was the best-preserved ancient Egyptian tomb ever uncovered. The tomb was filled with gold-covered furniture and other artifacts. In a special room in the tomb, Carter found a stone box with a series of golden coffins. They were stacked one inside another. Inside the last coffin was King Tut's mummy. The ancient Egyptians preserved people as mummies. They believed the dead would need their bodies in the afterlife.

4   Over the years, experts have come up with many theories, or ideas, about the cause of Tut's death. Some thought he died from an infection from a broken leg and a blood disease. Naunton decided to try to crack the case himself.

Mummy Mystery

5   Naunton began by looking back at Carter's notes. They described his discovery of Tut in 1922.

6   Carter's notes showed that Tut's mummy wasn't prepared like most other mummies. For one thing, his chest had been stuffed with linen and other materials. Naunton wondered why that might be.

7   So he examined X-ray images of Tut's skeleton that had been taken over the years. The images showed that Tut's heart and some of his ribs were missing. Naunton thought those parts must have been badly damaged. That might be why they were removed from his body before his burial. He thinks Tut's chest was stuffed with linen to keep it from collapsing.

8   The question was: What could have caused that much damage to Tut's ribs and heart?

(continued)

One of King Tut's coffins

Testing a Theory

9   Ancient Egyptian rulers often rode in horse-drawn chariots. Some experts had suggested in the past that Tut may have died in a chariot crash. Naunton had the same idea. So he decided to put that theory to the test.

10   Naunton worked with a group of car-crash investigators. They used computers to simulate a series of chariot accidents. They figured out that if a chariot had struck the young pharaoh in a certain way, it would have crushed his ribs and heart. Naunton believed he had his answer.

Case Closed?

11   Despite Naunton's experiment, many archaeologists don't agree with his theory. Some think Carter's team removed the ribs. That made it easier for them to carry the mummy out of the tomb. They also point out that Tut wasn't the only pharaoh to be found without his heart. Other archaeologists think Tut's ribs might have been damaged by another powerful force, like a kick from a horse.

12   Still, Naunton stands by his theory. "At this point, this is as good of a hypothesis that we have," he says. But, he adds, "I wouldn't want to think that this discussion is completely over."

HOW TO MAKE A MUMMY

The ancient Egyptians took about 70 days to prepare a body as a mummy. Only rulers and wealthy people got this treatment. Here's how it was done.

1. Remove the organs. The Egyptians usually left in the heart. Other organs were stored in special jars and buried with the mummy.

2. Add salt. Workers completely filled and covered the body with a type of salt, called natron. The natron dried out the body, helping to preserve it.

3. Wrap it up. After 40 days, workers washed the body and rubbed it with scented oils. Finally, they wrapped the body in strips of linen and placed it inside a special coffin, which was often decorated.

Name: _____

Directions: Read the article "Death of a Boy-King." Then answer the questions below.

1. What was the first step Chris Naunton took to try to figure out the cause of King Tut's death?

    A. He examined X-rays of King Tut's skeleton.

    B. He had car-crash investigators simulate chariot crashes.

    C. He had scans taken of King Tut's mummy.

    D. He studied the notes of the archaeologist who found Tut's tomb.

2. Which detail from the article best supports the answer to question 1?

    A. Naunton worked with a group of car-crash investigators. *(paragraph 10)*

    B. Naunton thought those parts must have been badly damaged. *(paragraph 7)*

    C. Naunton began by looking back at Carter's notes. *(paragraph 5)*

    D. So he examined X-ray images of Tut's skeleton that had been taken over the years. *(paragraph 7)*

3. What does the phrase "crack the case" mean as it is used in paragraph 4?

    A. Break open King Tut's coffin

    B. Solve the mystery of King Tut's death

    C. Work with car-crash investigators

    D. Accept an assignment to study Tut's mummy

4. According to the article, how did King Tut's mummy differ from most other Egyptian mummies?

    A. None of Tut's ribs were missing.

    B. It was placed in a special, decorated coffin.

    C. His heart was missing, and his chest was stuffed with linen and other materials.

    D. His chest was stuffed with salt and still had his heart.

5. Which detail from the section "How to Make a Mummy" best supports the answer to question 4?

    A. The Egyptians usually left in the heart.

    B. Other organs were stored in special jars and buried with the mummy.

    C. Finally, they . . . placed it inside a special coffin, which was often decorated.

    D. Workers completely filled and covered the body with a type of salt, called natron.

6. What is the section "Case Closed?" mostly about?

    A. How King Tut's tomb was discovered

    B. What scientists know about King Tut's life

    C. Why some scientists don't think King Tut was killed in a chariot accident

    D. How mummies were made in ancient Egypt

Name: _____

7. In paragraph 12, Chris Naunton says, "I wouldn't want to think that this discussion is completely over." What do you think he means by that statement? Give details to support your answer.

_____

_____

_____

_____

_____

_____

_____

_____

_____

Death of a Boy-King

1   King Tutankhamen (TOO-tahn-KAH-mehn) was just 9 years old when he became the ruler of Egypt. The young pharaoh died only 10 years later. That was more than 3,300 years ago. But his story has fascinated the world since his tomb was discovered in 1922.

2   Scientists have since learned a lot about Tut. But one thing has remained a mystery: How did he die? Chris Naunton, director of the Egypt Exploration Society, believes he may have solved the puzzle. He studied nearly 100 years' worth of evidence to come up with his answer. He thinks the boy-king was killed in a chariot accident.

A Golden Discovery

3   Not much was known about Tut for a long time. Then British archaeologist Howard Carter discovered Tut's tomb in Egypt. Filled with gold-covered furniture and other artifacts, it was the best-preserved ancient Egyptian tomb ever uncovered. In a special room in the tomb, Carter found a stone box with a series of golden coffins, stacked one inside another. Inside the last one was King Tut's mummy. The ancient Egyptians preserved people as mummies. They believed the dead would need their bodies in the afterlife.

4   Over the years, experts have come up with many theories, or ideas, about the cause of Tut's death. Some thought he died from an infection from a broken leg and a blood disease. Naunton decided to try to crack the case himself.

Mummy Mystery

5   Naunton began by looking back at Carter's notes describing his discovery of Tut in 1922.

6   "We wanted to see if there was anything in there that might be worth following up," Naunton told *Scholastic News*.

7   Carter's notes show that Tut's mummy wasn't prepared like most other mummies. For one thing, his chest had been stuffed with linen and other materials.

8   That led Naunton to examine X-ray images of Tut's skeleton that had been taken over the years. The images showed that the young pharaoh's heart and some of his ribs were missing. Naunton thought these parts must have been badly damaged. That's why they were removed from Tut's body before his burial. He thinks Tut's chest was stuffed with linen to keep it from collapsing.

9   The question was: What could have caused that much damage to Tut's ribs and heart?

(continued)

One of King
Tut's coffins

Testing a Theory

10   Ancient Egyptian rulers often rode in horse-drawn chariots while hunting or during battles. In the past, some experts had suggested that Tut may have died in a chariot crash. Naunton had the same idea. So he decided to put that theory to the test.

11   Naunton asked a group of car-crash investigators to use computers to simulate a series of chariot accidents. They determined that if a chariot had struck the young pharaoh in a certain way, it would have crushed his ribs and heart. Naunton believed he had his answer.

Case Closed?

12   Despite Naunton's experiment, many archaeologists don't agree with his theory. Some say Tut's ribs didn't go missing from his body until thousands of years after his death. They think Carter's team removed the ribs. That would make it easier for them to carry the mummy out of the tomb. They also point out that Tut wasn't the only pharaoh to be found without his heart. Other archaeologists think Tut's ribs might have been damaged by another powerful force, like a kick from a horse.

13   Still, Naunton stands by his theory. "At this point, this is as good of a hypothesis that we have," he says. But, he adds, "I wouldn't want to think that this discussion is completely over."

HOW TO MAKE A MUMMY

The ancient Egyptians took about 70 days to prepare a body as a mummy. Only rulers and wealthy people got this treatment. Here's how it was done.

1. Remove the organs. The Egyptians usually left in the heart. Other organs were stored in special jars and buried with the mummy.

2. Add salt. Workers completely filled and covered the body with a type of salt, called natron. The natron dried out the body, helping to preserve it.

3. Wrap it up. After 40 days, workers washed the body and rubbed it with scented oils. Finally, they wrapped the body in strips of linen and placed it inside a special coffin, which was often decorated.

Name: _____

Directions: Read the article "Death of a Boy-King." Then answer the questions below.

1. What was the first step Chris Naunton took to try to figure out the cause of King Tut's death?

    A. He examined X-rays of King Tut's skeleton.

    B. He had car-crash investigators simulate chariot crashes.

    C. He studied the notes of the archaeologist who found Tut's tomb.

    D. He had scans taken of King Tut's mummy.

2. Which detail from the article best supports the answer to question 1?

    A. That led Naunton to examine X-ray images of Tut's skeleton that had been taken over the years. *(paragraph 8)*

    B. Naunton thought these parts must have been badly damaged. *(paragraph 8)*

    C. Naunton asked a group of car-crash investigators to use computers to simulate a series of chariot accidents. *(paragraph 11)*

    D. Naunton began by looking back at Carter's notes describing his discovery of Tut in 1922. *(paragraph 5)*

3. What does the phrase "crack the case" mean as it is used in paragraph 4?

    A. Solve the mystery of King Tut's death

    B. Work with car-crash investigators

    C. Break open King Tut's coffin

    D. Accept an assignment to study Tut's mummy

4. According to the article, how did King Tut's mummy differ from most other Egyptian mummies?

    A. It was placed in a special, decorated coffin.

    B. None of Tut's ribs were missing.

    C. His chest was stuffed with salt and still had his heart.

    D. His heart was missing, and his chest was stuffed with linen and other materials.

5. Which detail from the sidebar "How to Make a Mummy" best supports the answer to question 4?

    A. Other organs were stored in special jars and buried with the mummy.

    B. The Egyptians usually left in the heart.

    C. Finally, they . . . placed it inside a special coffin, which was often decorated.

    D. Workers completely filled and covered the body with a type of salt, called natron.

6. What is the section "Case Closed?" mostly about?

    A. What scientists know about King Tut's life

    B. Why some scientists don't think King Tut was killed in a chariot accident

    C. How mummies were made in ancient Egypt

    D. How King Tut's tomb was discovered

Name: _____

7. In paragraph 13, Chris Naunton says, "I wouldn't want to think that this discussion
   is completely over." What do you think he means by that statement? Give details
   to support your answer.

_____

_____

_____

_____

_____

_____

_____

_____

_____

_____

Journey to the Bottom of the Sea

1   Some of the strangest creatures on the planet live in the deep sea. They live in a world with no sunlight. The seawater is bitter cold.

2   I once visited this strange world. It was the most exciting trip of my life! I traveled a mile and a half to the bottom of the Pacific Ocean in a **submersible** called *Alvin*. Scientists have been using this underwater vehicle to observe the ocean for more than 50 years. They even used it to explore the shipwreck of the *Titanic* in 1986.

3   *Alvin* recently got several upgrades. The sub has many new features, such as improved cameras and robotic arms. Scientist Stefan Sievert set out to visit the seafloor in *Alvin*. And I got to go with him!

Into the Water

4   We sailed from Mexico into the Pacific aboard a research ship. It took us three days to reach the study site. At the site was a group of openings in the seafloor called hydrothermal vents. Warm fluids flow out of these vents. Scientists were researching life near there.

5   Early one morning, I climbed into *Alvin* with Sievert and pilot Phil Forte. Our trip to the seafloor was smooth and quiet. We watched through the windows as the water changed from green to blue to black. Near the bottom, Forte turned on the lights. At first, we saw only the seafloor's shiny black rock. But soon we reached the vents. Animals, such as worms, fish, and crabs, swam around the vents.

6   Tiny creatures called microbes also live at the vents. They make their own food from vent fluids. Microbes form the base of the food web here, just like plants do on land. Many animals survive down here by eating the microbes.

Tube worms

At the Seafloor

7   At one vent, Sievert said, "You've got to see this." Outside his window was a tower of tube worms. There must have been thousands of them!

8   Tube worms can grow to be more than 6 feet long. They have no eyes, no mouth, and no stomach. Microbes live in their bodies and make food for them.

9   Next, we saw a vent called a black smoker. The thick black fluid that flows from this type of vent is very hot—more than 660°F! Small worms that live there can survive extremely high temperatures.

10 The day flew by as we explored. Finally, after six hours, Forte said, "Time to get going." I wish we could have stayed longer!

—by Jen Barone

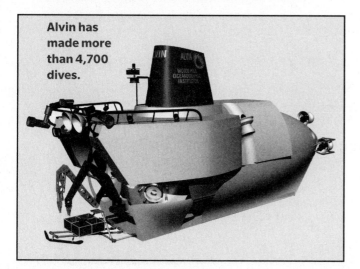

Alvin has made more than 4,700 dives.

Name: _____

Directions: Read the article "Journey to the Bottom of the Sea."
Then answer the questions below.

1. **Which of the following best states the main idea of the article?**

   A. *Alvin* recently got several upgrades.

   B. Scientists explored the deep sea in *Alvin* to learn about the strange creatures that live there.

   C. Hydrothermal vents are openings in the seafloor where warm fluids escape.

   D. Animals living on the seafloor are very different from those that live on land.

2. **Based on the article, which of the following is the best definition for *submersible*?**

   A. A vehicle that recently got upgrades

   B. A vehicle used for very long trips

   C. An underwater vehicle

   D. A vehicle designed to explore hydrothermal vents

3. **Why does the author mention the *Titanic* in paragraph 2?**

   A. To give an example of an important expedition *Alvin* has made

   B. To compare its features with those of *Alvin*

   C. To explain why she was invited to explore the deep sea

   D. To describe one of the exciting things she saw during her trip

4. **Which sentence from the article suggests that the author enjoyed her trip to the seafloor?**

   A. We sailed from Mexico into the Pacific aboard a research ship. *(paragraph 4)*

   B. I once visited this strange world. *(paragraph 2)*

   C. I wish we could have stayed longer! *(paragraph 10)*

   D. Early one morning, I climbed into *Alvin* with Sievert and pilot Phil Forte. *(paragraph 5)*

5. **According to the article, how are microbes living near hydrothermal vents similar to plants on land?**

   A. They are both at the base of the food web.

   B. They both need sunlight to survive.

   C. They both need hydrothermal vents to survive.

   D. They both can survive in strange environments.

6. **Which choice best describes the relationship between tube worms and microbes?**

   A. Tube worms eat microbes.

   B. Tube worms make food for microbes.

   C. Microbes and tube worms compete for food.

   D. Tube worms depend on microbes for food.

Name: _____

7. In paragraph 1, the author states that the deep sea is home to some of the strangest creatures on the planet. How does the section "At the Seafloor" support this idea? Use at least two details from that section in your answer.

_____

_____

_____

_____

8. Which of the following can be inferred from the article?
   A. Hydrothermal vents are difficult to spot.
   B. Hydrothermal vents provide resources that deep-sea creatures need to survive.
   C. Scientists discovered hydrothermal vents for the first time while exploring the deep sea in *Alvin*.
   D. Hydrothermal vents are dangerous for creatures living in the deep sea.

9. Which sentence from the article best supports the answer to question 8?
   A. At first, we saw only the seafloor's shiny black rock. *(paragraph 5)*
   B. It took us three days to reach the study site. *(paragraph 4)*
   C. The thick black fluid that flows from this type of vent is very hot—more than 660°F! *(paragraph 9)*
   D. Animals, such as worms, fish, and crabs, swam around the vents. *(paragraph 5)*

10. In paragraph 10, the author uses the phrase "The day flew by." What does this phrase suggest?
   A. Time seemed to pass quickly while she was exploring the deep sea.
   B. *Alvin* moved through the ocean at a very high speed.
   C. She spent very little time at the bottom of the ocean.
   D. She didn't pay much attention to what happened during the day.

11. According to the article, what makes the deep sea an unusual place for life? What helps creatures survive there? Use details from the article to support your answer.

_____

_____

_____

_____

Journey to the Bottom of the Sea

1 The deep sea is home to some of the most unusual creatures on the planet. They live in a world with no sunlight. The seawater is a bitter-cold 36.5 degrees Fahrenheit (36.5°F).

2 In November 2014, I visited this strange world. It was the most exciting trip of my life: a mile-and-a-half journey to the bottom of the Pacific Ocean. A **submersible** called *Alvin* took me there. Scientists have been using this underwater vehicle to observe the ocean for more than 50 years. It was even used to explore the shipwreck of the *Titanic* in 1986.

3 *Alvin* recently got several upgrades. The sub has many new features, including improved cameras and robotic arms. Scientist Stefan Sievert set out to visit the Pacific seafloor in *Alvin*, and I was lucky enough to get a chance to go with him.

Into the Water

4 We sailed from Mexico into the eastern Pacific aboard the research ship *Atlantis.* It took us three days to reach the study site—a group of openings in the seafloor called hydrothermal vents. Warm fluids flow out of these vents. The scientists were researching life near there.

5 On the morning of my dive in *Alvin*, I climbed into the sub with Sievert and pilot

Alvin has made more than 4,700 dives.

Phil Forte. Our trip to the seafloor was smooth and quiet. We watched through the windows as the water changed from green to blue to black. Near the bottom, Forte turned on the lights. At first, we saw only the seafloor's shiny black rock. But soon we reached the vents. They were surrounded by animals, including worms, fish, and crabs.

6 Tiny creatures called microbes also live at the vents. They make their own food from vent fluids. Microbes form the base of the food web here, just like plants do on land. Many animals survive at these great depths by eating the microbes.

Tube worms

At the Seafloor

7 At one vent, Sievert motioned to me. "You've got to see this," he said. Outside his window was a tower of tube worms so tall that I couldn't even see the top. There must have been thousands of them.

8 Tube worms can grow to be more than 6 feet long. They have no eyes, no mouth, and no stomach. Microbes live in a pouch in the tube worms' bodies and make food for them.

9 Next, we saw a vent called a black smoker. The thick black fluid that flows from this type of vent is very hot—more than 660°F! Small worms that live there can survive extremely high temperatures.

10 The day flew by as we explored. Finally, after six hours, Forte said, "Time to get going." I wish we could have stayed longer!

—by Jen Barone

Name: _____

Directions: Read the article "Journey to the Bottom of the Sea." Then answer the questions below.

1. Which of the following best states the main idea of the article?

A. *Alvin* recently got several upgrades.

B. Hydrothermal vents are openings in the seafloor where hot fluid escapes.

C. Animals living on the seafloor are very different from those that live on land.

D. Scientists explore the deep sea in *Alvin* to learn about the strange creatures that live there.

2. Based on the article, which of the following is the best definition for *submersible*?

A. An underwater vehicle

B. A vehicle that recently got upgrades

C. A vehicle used for very long trips

D. A vehicle designed to explore hydrothermal vents

3. Why does the author mention the *Titanic* in paragraph 2?

A. To compare its features with those of *Alvin*

B. To give an example of an important expedition *Alvin* has made

C. To describe one of the exciting things she saw during her trip

D. To explain why she was invited to explore the deep sea

4. Which sentence from the article suggests that the author enjoyed her trip to the seafloor?

A. In November 2014, I visited this strange world. *(paragraph 2)*

B. We sailed from Mexico into the eastern Pacific aboard the research ship *Atlantis*. *(paragraph 4)*

C. On the morning of my dive in *Alvin*, I climbed into the sub with Sievert and pilot Phil Forte. *(paragraph 5)*

D. I wish we could have stayed longer! *(paragraph 10)*

5. According to the article, how are microbes living near hydrothermal vents similar to plants on land?

A. They both need sunlight to survive.

B. They both need hydrothermal vents to survive.

C. They are both at the bottom of the food web.

D. They both can survive in strange environments.

6. Which choice best describes the relationship between tube worms and microbes?

A. Tube worms eat microbes.

B. Tube worms make food for microbes.

C. Tube worms depend on microbes for food.

D. Microbes and tube worms compete for food.

Name: _____

7. In paragraph 1, the author states that the deep sea is home to some of the most unusual creatures on the planet. How does the section "At the Seafloor" support this idea? Use at least two details from that section in your answer.

_____

_____

_____

_____

8. Which of the following can be inferred from the article?

   A. Scientists discovered hydrothermal vents for the first time while exploring the deep sea in *Alvin*.

   B. Hydrothermal vents are dangerous for creatures living in the deep sea.

   C. Hydrothermal vents provide resources that deep-sea creatures need to survive.

   D. Hydrothermal vents are difficult to spot.

9. Which sentence from the article best supports the answer to question 8?

   A. It took us three days to reach the study site—a group of openings in the seafloor called hydrothermal vents. *(paragraph 4)*

   B. At first, we saw only the seafloor's shiny black rock. *(paragraph 5)*

   C. They were surrounded by animals, including worms, fish, and crabs. *(paragraph 5)*

   D. The thick black fluid that flows from this type of vent is very hot—more than 660°F! *(paragraph 9)*

10. In paragraph 10, the author uses the phrase "The day flew by." What does this phrase suggest?

   A. She spent very little time at the bottom of the ocean.

   B. *Alvin* moved through the ocean at a very high speed.

   C. Time seemed to pass quickly while she was exploring the deep sea.

   D. She didn't pay much attention to what happened during the day.

11. According to the article, what makes the deep sea an unusual place for life? What helps creatures survive there? Use details from the article to support your answer.

_____

_____

_____

_____

Journey to the Bottom of the Sea

1   The deep sea is home to some of the most unusual creatures on the planet. They live in a world with no sunlight, with the seawater a bitter-cold 36.5 degrees Fahrenheit (36.5°F).

2   In November 2014, I visited this strange world. It was the most exciting trip of my life—a mile-and-a-half journey to the bottom of the Pacific Ocean. A **submersible** called *Alvin* took me there. Scientists have been using this underwater vehicle to observe the ocean for more than 50 years. It was even used to explore the shipwreck of the *Titanic* in 1986.

3   *Alvin* recently got several upgrades, including improved cameras and robotic arms. Eager to try out these upgrades, scientist Stefan Sievert set out to visit the Pacific seafloor in *Alvin*. And I was lucky enough to get a chance to go with him.

Into the Water

4   We sailed from Mexico into the eastern Pacific aboard the research ship *Atlantis*. It took us three days to reach the study site—a group of openings in the seafloor called hydrothermal vents, from which warm fluids flow. Scientists wanted to learn more about organisms that live near these vents.

Alvin has made more than 4,700 dives.

5   On the morning of my dive in *Alvin*, I climbed into the sub with Sievert and pilot Phil Forte. Our trip to the seafloor was smooth and quiet. We watched through the windows as the water changed from green to blue to black. Near the bottom, Forte turned on the lights. At first, we saw only the seafloor's shiny black rock. But soon we reached the vents. They were surrounded by animals, including worms, fish, and crabs.

6   Tiny creatures called microbes also live at the vents. They make their own food from vent fluids. Microbes form the base of the food web here, just like plants do on land. Many animals survive at these great depths by eating the microbes.

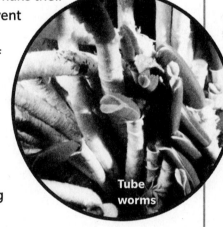

Tube worms

At the Seafloor

7   At one vent, Sievert motioned to me. "You've got to see this," he said. Outside his window was a tower of tube worms so tall, I couldn't even see the top. There must have been thousands of them.

8   Tube worms can grow to be more than 6 feet long. They have no eyes, no mouth, and no stomach. Microbes live in a pouch in the tube worms' bodies and make food for them.

9   Next, we saw a vent called a black smoker. The thick black fluid that flows from this type of vent is very hot—more than 660°F! Small worms that live there can survive extremely high temperatures.

10   The day flew by as we explored. Finally, after six hours, Forte said, "Time to get going." I wish we could have stayed longer!

—by Jen Barone

Name: _____

Directions: Read the article "Journey to the Bottom of the Sea."
Then answer the questions below.

1. Which of the following best states the main idea of the article?

    A. Hydrothermal vents are openings in the seafloor where hot fluid escapes.

    B. *Alvin* recently got several upgrades.

    C. Scientists explore the deep sea in *Alvin* to learn about the strange creatures that live there.

    D. Animals living on the seafloor are very different from those that live on land.

2. Based on the article, which of the following is the best definition for *submersible*?

    A. A vehicle that recently got upgrades

    B. An underwater vehicle

    C. A vehicle used for very long trips

    D. A vehicle designed to explore hydrothermal vents

3. Why does the author mention the *Titanic* in paragraph 2?

    A. To compare its features with those of *Alvin*

    B. To describe one of the exciting things she saw during her trip

    C. To give an example of an important expedition *Alvin* has made

    D. To explain why she was invited to explore the deep sea

4. Which sentence from the article suggests that the author enjoyed her trip to the seafloor?

    A. I wish we could have stayed longer! *(paragraph 10)*

    B. On the morning of my dive in *Alvin*, I climbed into the sub with Sievert and pilot Phil Forte. *(paragraph 5)*

    C. In November 2014, I visited this strange world. *(paragraph 2)*

    D. We sailed from Mexico into the eastern Pacific aboard the research ship *Atlantis*. *(paragraph 4)*

5. According to the article, how are microbes living near hydrothermal vents similar to plants on land?

    A. They both need hydrothermal vents to survive.

    B. They are both at the bottom of the food web.

    C. They both can survive in strange environments.

    D. They both need sunlight to survive.

6. Which choice best describes the relationship between tube worms and microbes?

    A. Tube worms depend on microbes for food.

    B. Tube worms eat microbes.

    C. Tube worms make food for microbes.

    D. Microbes and tube worms compete for food.

Name: _____

7. In paragraph 1, the author states that the deep sea is home to some of the most unusual creatures on the planet. How does the section "At the Seafloor" support this idea? Use at least two details from that section in your answer.

_____

_____

_____

_____

8. Which of the following can be inferred from the article?

   A. Scientists discovered hydrothermal vents for the first time while exploring the deep sea in *Alvin*.

   B. Hydrothermal vents provide resources that deep-sea creatures need to survive.

   C. Hydrothermal vents are dangerous for creatures living in the deep sea.

   D. Hydrothermal vents are difficult to spot.

9. Which sentence from the article best supports the answer to question 7?

   A. They were surrounded by animals, including worms, fish, and crabs. *(paragraph 5)*

   B. It took us three days to reach the study site—a group of openings in the seafloor called hydrothermal vents . . . *(paragraph 4)*

   C. At first, we saw only the seafloor's shiny black rock. *(paragraph 5)*

   D. The thick black fluid that flows from this type of vent is very hot—more than 660°F! *(paragraph 9)*

10. In paragraph 10, the author uses the phrase "The day flew by." What does this phrase suggest?

   A. She spent very little time at the bottom of the ocean.

   B. *Alvin* moved through the ocean at a very high speed.

   C. She didn't pay much attention to what happened during the day.

   D. Time seemed to pass quickly while she was exploring the deep sea.

11. According to the article, what makes the deep sea an unusual place for life? What helps creatures survive there? Use details from the article to support your answer.

_____

_____

_____

_____

Answer Key

SCHOOL ON A BUS

page 7
1. b **2.** Answers will vary. Sample response: *Buses are equipped with supplies and teachers. They keep students from having to travel far to get to school.* **3.** available – scarce; recent – historic; poverty – wealth **4.** a **5.** d

page 9
1. d **2.** Answers will vary. Sample response: *Buses are equipped with supplies and teachers. They keep students from having to travel far to get to school.* **3.** poverty – wealth; recent – historic; available – scarce **4.** b **5.** c

page 11
1. a **2.** Answers will vary. Sample response: *Buses are equipped with supplies and teachers. They keep students from having to travel far to get to school.* **3.** recent – historic; poverty – wealth; available – scarce **4.** c **5.** a

A DYNAMIC DUO

page 14
1. c **2.** a **3.** b **4.** c **5.** d

page 17
1. a **2.** b **3.** a **4.** d **5.** b

page 20
1. b **2.** c **3.** d **4.** a **5.** c

DON'T JUST STAND BY

page 22
1. c **2.** a **3.** d **4.** b **5.** a **6.** Answers will vary. Sample response: *Nathalie was bullied for many years. The bully bossed her around and spread rumors about her. The bully even pushed her into a trash can. The situation was resolved when another student stood up to the bully.*

page 24
1. b **2.** d **3.** a **4.** c **5.** c **6.** Answers will vary. Sample response: *Nathalie was bullied for many years. The bully bossed her around and spread rumors about her. The bully even pushed her into a trash can. The situation was resolved when another student stood up to the bully.*

page 26
1. a **2.** b **3.** c **4.** a **5.** b **6.** Answers will vary. Sample response: *Nathalie was bullied for many years. The bully bossed her around and spread rumors about her. The bully even pushed her into a trash can. The situation was resolved when another student stood up to the bully.*

FOR SALE: VOLCANIC POWER

page 28
1. c **2.** a **3.** d **4.** Answers will vary. Sample response: *Cause: Volcanic activity in Iceland creates pools of steamy water called hot springs. Effect: Iceland can sell renewable energy to other European countries.* **5.** b **6.** a

page 30
1. d **2.** b **3.** a **4.** Answers will vary. Sample response: *Cause: Volcanic activity in Iceland creates pools of steamy water called hot springs. Effect: Iceland can sell renewable energy to other European countries.* **5.** d **6.** c

page 32
1. a **2.** d **3.** c **4.** Answers will vary. Sample response: *Cause: Volcanic activity in Iceland creates pools of steamy water called hot springs. Effect: Iceland can sell renewable energy to other European countries.* **5.** a **6.** d

CHINA'S ANCIENT ARMY

page 34
1. a **2.** c **3.** a **4.** d **5.** b **6.** Answers will vary. Sample response: *In the section "Hidden Tomb," the author reveals that much of Qin's tomb has yet to be uncovered. For example, she states that archaeologists believe about 6,000 more statues—as well as the body of the emperor—could still be deep underground. The author also informs the reader that according to legend, "Qin's tomb is booby-trapped to keep people away." Based on these details, I can infer that Qin did not want anyone inside his tomb. Otherwise, he would not have made it so difficult for people to discover it.*

page 36
1. c **2.** b **3.** d **4.** b **5.** a **6.** Answers will vary. Sample response: *In the section "Hidden Tomb," the*

author reveals that much of Qin's tomb has yet to be uncovered. For example, she states that archaeologists believe about 6,000 more statues—as well as the body of the emperor—could still be deep underground. She also informs the reader that according to legend, "Qin's tomb is booby-trapped to keep people away." Based on these details, I can infer that Qin did not want anyone inside his tomb. Otherwise, he would not have made it so difficult for people to discover it.

page 38
1. b **2.** a **3.** c **4.** c **5.** d **6.** Answers will vary. Sample response: *In the section "Hidden Tomb," the author reveals that much of Qin's tomb has yet to be uncovered. For example, she states that archaeologists believe about 6,000 more statues—as well as the body of the emperor—could still be deep underground. She also informs the reader that according to legend, "Qin's tomb is booby-trapped with arrows to keep people from entering." Based on these details, I can infer that Qin did not want anyone inside his tomb. Otherwise, he would not have made it so difficult for people to discover it.*

A MODERN-DAY GOLD RUSH
page 40
1. b **2.** d **3.** c **4.** a **5.** Answers will vary. Sample response: *Cause: People heard about a gold nugget found at Sutter's Mill. Effect: The population of California grew as people arrived there and opened inns, banks, and other businesses.* **6.** a

page 42
1. c **2.** c **3.** d **4.** b **5.** Answers will vary. Sample response: *Cause: People heard about a gold nugget found at Sutter's Mill. Effect: The population of California grew as people arrived there and opened inns, banks, and other businesses.* **6.** d

page 44
1. a **2.** b **3.** a **4.** d **5.** Answers will vary. Sample response: *Cause: People heard about a gold nugget found at Sutter's Mill. Effect: The population of California grew as people arrived there and opened inns, banks, and other businesses.* **6.** b

POWERFUL WORDS
page 46
1. b **2.** c **3.** a **4.** c **5.** d **6.** Answers will vary. Sample response: *The Battle of Gettysburg was important because it was a turning point in the Civil War.*

The Union victory forced the Confederate Army back into the South. The Gettysburg Address was a key event because it honored the soldiers who died in the Battle of Gettysburg. In the speech, Lincoln talked about why it was important for the Union to win the war.

page 48
1. c **2.** a **3.** d **4.** d **5.** c **6.** Answers will vary. Sample response: *The Battle of Gettysburg was important because it was a turning point in the Civil War. The Union victory forced the Confederate Army back into the South. The Gettysburg Address was a key event because it honored the soldiers who died in the Battle of Gettysburg. In the speech, Lincoln talked about why it was important for the Union to win the war.*

page 50
1. d **2.** d **3.** b **4.** b **5.** a **6.** Answers will vary. Sample response: *The Battle of Gettysburg was important because it was a turning point in the Civil War. The Union victory forced the Confederate Army back into the South. The Gettysburg Address was a key event because it honored the soldiers who died in the Battle of Gettysburg. In the speech, Lincoln talked about why it was important for the Union to win the war.*

SEARCHING FOR AMELIA
page 52
1. 2, 4, 3, 1 **2.** Answers will vary. Sample response: *Researchers found artifacts that they think belonged to Amelia Earhart. They also believe a photo shows part of her plane sticking out of the water. Another image from the ocean floor shows what appears to be an airplane wing.* **3.** c **4.** d **5.** a **6.** b

page 54
1. 1, 3, 4, 2 **2.** Answers will vary. Sample response: *Researchers found artifacts that they think belonged to Amelia Earhart. They also believe a photo shows part of her plane sticking out of the water. Another image from the ocean floor shows what appears to be an airplane wing.* **3.** c **4.** a **5.** d **6.** Answers will vary. Sample response: *The subheadings organize the information by topics related to the search for Earhart.* **7.** a

page 56
1. 3, 2, 4, 1 **2.** Answers will vary. Sample response: *Researchers found artifacts that they think belonged to Amelia Earhart. They also believe a photo shows part of her plane sticking out of the water. Another image from*

the ocean floor shows what appears to be an airplane wing. **3.** a **4.** c **5.** c **6.** Answers will vary. Sample response: *The subheadings organize the information by topics related to the search for Earhart.* **7.** c

DEATH OF A BOY-KING
page 59
1. b **2.** a **3.** c **4.** a **5.** c **6.** d **7.** Answers will vary. Sample response: *Chris Naunton means that he hopes scientists will continue to try to figure out what killed King Tut. Even though Naunton believes that a chariot accident caused Tut's death, he describes it as "as good of a hypothesis that we have." So the mystery doesn't seem to be officially solved. In fact, in the section "Case Closed?" the author states that many archaeologists disagree with Naunton. The author describes other theories about what could have caused the damage to Tut's body. For example, some scientists think Carter removed the ribs to make it easier to carry the mummy out of the tomb.*

page 63
1. d **2.** c **3.** b **4.** c **5.** a **6.** c **7.** Answers will vary. Sample response: *Chris Naunton means that he hopes scientists will continue to try to figure out what killed King Tut. Even though Naunton believes that a chariot accident caused Tut's death, he describes it as "as good of a hypothesis that we have." So the mystery doesn't seem to be officially solved. In fact, in the section "Case Closed?" the author states that many archaeologists disagree with Naunton. The author describes other theories about what could have caused the damage to Tut's body. For example, some scientists think Carter removed the ribs to make it easier to carry the mummy out of the tomb.*

page 67
1. c **2.** d **3.** a **4.** d **5.** b **6.** b **7.** Answers will vary. Sample response: *Chris Naunton means that he hopes scientists will continue to try to figure out what killed King Tut. Even though Naunton believes that a chariot accident caused Tut's death, he describes it as "as good of a hypothesis that we have." So the mystery doesn't seem to be officially solved. In fact, in the section "Case Closed?" the author states that many archaeologists disagree with Naunton. The author describes other theories about what could have caused the damage to Tut's body. For example, some scientists*

think Carter removed the ribs to make it easier to carry the mummy out of the tomb.

JOURNEY TO THE BOTTOM OF THE SEA
page 70
1. b **2.** c **3.** a **4.** c **5.** a **6.** d **7.** Answers will vary. Sample response: *The section "At the Seafloor" describes some of the unusual creatures that live in the deep sea. For example, tube worms have no eyes, no mouth, and no stomach. And small worms that live near black smoker vents can survive extremely high temperatures.* **8.** b **9.** d **10.** a **11.** Answers will vary. Sample response: *The deep sea is a harsh environment for life because there is no sunlight and it's very cold. Creatures survive there thanks to hydrothermal vents. The vents provide resources that microbes need to make food. Other creatures eat the microbes.*

page 73
1. d **2.** a **3.** b **4.** d **5.** c **6.** c **7.** Answers will vary. Sample response: *The section "At the Seafloor" describes some of the unusual creatures that live in the deep sea. For example, tube worms have no eyes, no mouth, and no stomach. And small worms that live near black smoker vents can survive extremely high temperatures.* **8.** c **9.** c **10.** c **11.** Answers will vary. Sample response: *The deep sea is a harsh environment for life because there is no sunlight and it's very cold. Creatures survive there thanks to hydrothermal vents. The vents provide resources that microbes need to make food. Other creatures eat the microbes.*

page 76
1. c **2.** b **3.** c **4.** a **5.** b **6.** a **7.** Answers will vary. Sample response: *The section "At the Seafloor" describes some of the unusual creatures that live in the deep sea. For example, tube worms have no eyes, no mouth, and no stomach. And small worms that live near black smoker vents can survive extremely high temperatures.* **8.** b **9.** a **10.** d **11.** Answers will vary. Sample response: *The deep sea is a harsh environment for life because there is no sunlight and it's very cold. Creatures survive there thanks to hydrothermal vents. The vents provide resources that microbes need to make food. Other creatures eat the microbes.*